Understanding
Depression

Dr Kwame McKenzie

Published by Family Doctor Publications Limited
in association with the British Medical Association

IMPORTANT

This book is intended not as a substitute for personal medical advice but as a supplement to that advice for the patient who wishes to understand more about his or her condition.

Before taking any form of treatment
YOU SHOULD ALWAYS CONSULT YOUR MEDICAL PRACTITIONER.

In particular (without limit) you should note that advances in medical science occur rapidly and some information about drugs and treatment contained in this booklet may very soon be out of date.

© Family Doctor Publications 1998–2006
Updated 1999, 2000, 2001, 2002, 2003, 2004, 2006

Family Doctor Publications, PO Box 4664, Poole, Dorset BH15 1NN

ISBN: 1 903474 35 3

Contents

About the author

Dr Kwame McKenzie is a Senior Lecturer and Consultant Psychiatrist at the Royal Free Hospital and University College Medical School in London. He is committed to improving the understanding of mental illness and has written over 200 articles, hosted a TV series and conducted numerous radio interviews on the subject.

Introduction

What is depression?

We all have low moods from time to time. For instance, if a relationship breaks up we may feel shocked, we may cry, go off our food, get angry and irritable, sleep poorly, and get tetchy and anxious. Usually, the mood passes after a few days and we get back to our normal way of living. We may say that we have been 'depressed', 'down in the dumps', 'fed up' or have had the 'blues'.

But low moods like this are not what doctors call depression. Instead, they use the term to describe a more severe illness that a person has had for at least a few weeks, affecting the body as well as the mind. It can come on for no reason at all and may sometimes be life threatening. No one symptom indicates whether you have just a low mood or what some people call 'clinical depression'. Many of the symptoms are similar; however, when you are depressed they are usually more intense and go on for longer.

A simple rule of thumb is that, if your low mood affects all parts of your life, lasts for two weeks or brings you to the point of thinking about suicide, you should seek help. Try to remember that depression is an illness that can be treated and you will feel better in time.

Ninety per cent of people with depression are treated by their GP and you shouldn't worry that he or she will think it a sign of weakness. Family doctors have years of experience in dealing with depression and are trained to diagnose and treat it. They may prescribe tablets, but will probably also tell you about self-help organisations, counselling and psychotherapy or relaxation techniques. You may get advice on ways of decreasing your stress or coming to terms with a bereavement or other loss. GPs are a mine of information.

But if you do not feel that you can talk to your doctor, talk with a friend. You will be surprised how many people have experience of depression either first hand or because they know someone who has been depressed. They may be able to give you support and advice but, even if they just listen, talking to someone usually helps.

How common is depression?

Many famous people have suffered from depression, including Abraham Lincoln, Queen Victoria and Winston Churchill, who called depression his 'black dog'.

Many writers and actors have suffered from depression and the comedian Spike Milligan wrote a book about his depressive illness, *Depression and How to Survive It*.

Facts about depression

- At least one in five adults will suffer from depression in their lifetime.
- Each year doctors diagnose two million cases in the UK.
- On average, each GP in the UK sees one patient with depression a day.
- Depression affects all age groups.
- Women are diagnosed as suffering from it twice as often as men.

There has been an increase in the rates of depression over the last 40 years which may be the result of the way we live our lives now. For many people, the world is becoming increasingly stressful and stress can lead to depression. Increases in divorce rates and crime rates, longer working hours for some and unemployment for others are just some of the factors that make life a strain for those affected.

Where we live may be important for our risk of depression too. One study showed that people who live in an inner-city area are twice as likely to be depressed as those who live in the Hebrides. Although it has proved difficult to find an exact reason for this, it is clear that your environment is important to your risk of depression.

The good news is that no matter what the cause of depression it can be treated and treated effectively. Most people who are depressed and get treatment get better.

KEY POINTS

- Low moods are thought of as depression if they persist and affect all parts of your life

- Depression is common

- Depression can be treated effectively

What is depression?

An illness of mind and body

Depression is an illness of mind and body. Most people have both physical and psychological symptoms, but their exact nature will vary from one person to another. Different symptoms will be more or less prominent in each person's illness. Some people report no symptoms at all but begin behaving in an unusual way – for example, one previously law-abiding woman who came to my clinic had started shop-lifting when she became depressed.

Psychological symptoms
Low mood

Despite the use of the label depression, not everyone with this illness feels low. Some are anxious, some say they are emotionally numb and some have no mood changes but come to their doctor with unexplained physical symptoms or with a change in behaviour.

Low mood in depression is much more intense than the way you feel when you are disappointed or just

Symptoms of depression

Depression has a wide range of possible psychological and physical symptoms. What one person experiences as symptoms of depression may well be very different to what another person experiences.

Psychological

- Low mood
- Loss of interest in things you used to enjoy
- Anxiety
- Emotional numbness
- Depressive thinking
- Concentration and memory problems
- Delusions
- Hallucinations
- Suicidal impulse

Physical

- Sleep problems – difficulty getting to sleep, waking up early or sleeping too much
- Mental and physical slowing
- Increase or decrease in appetite
- Increase or decrease in weight
- Loss of interest in sex
- Tiredness
- Constipation
- Menstrual period irregularities

fed up. It is a persistent feeling of sadness, emptiness, loss and dread. Some say it is like living with a cloud over you and it takes over every part of your life.

Diurnal variations
In moderate or severe depression, low mood is often worse in the morning and improves slightly during the day – though it never goes. This is called diurnal variation.

Anhedonia
Low mood makes it impossible to enjoy anything and you may even lose interest in your hobbies. Nothing brings you pleasure. Doctors call this symptom anhedonia.

In some milder depressions low mood may be worse in the evenings than in the mornings and there may be the odd good day. However, these are outnumbered by the bad ones. If depression is mild you may be able to enjoy other people's company – though without stimulation you would soon become disenchanted again.

With the low mood comes a tendency to cry more often, with the slightest upset or even with no upset at all.

Anxiety
When we feel threatened, a hormone called adrenaline is released and blood is directed to our muscles and brain so that we can think quickly and flee if we need to. We feel on edge, jumpy and tense but, if nothing happens, the feeling passes off in a few minutes. In someone who is depressed, these anxious feelings can last for months.

Some people wake in the morning in a state of high anxiety because they dread the day ahead. Anxiety can outweigh low mood and be the most prominent

symptom in depression. If you are in a state of anxiety you may find that you get irritable and snap a lot which is obviously difficult for other people to live with as well as for you.

Emotional numbness
Some people who are severely depressed say that they feel like they have completely lost their emotions and this is one of the most distressing symptoms of depression. You feel numb. You can't cry and you feel like there are no tears left. You may not feel that you are part of the world because you do not think that you have feelings. You may feel distant and unfeeling about even people very close to you such as your partner, family or children.

Depressive thinking
Your thinking changes when you are suffering from depression. You see the world differently and

everything appears in a negative light. This distorted view simply reinforces the depression.

You may blame yourself for unfortunate events more than you should while not allowing yourself to take credit for things that you have done well. The good things that you have done throughout your life are forgotten and the bad are vividly remembered and blown up out of all proportion.

You may find yourself concentrating on the negative detail and ignoring the bigger picture. To take an extreme example, someone who had passed an exam with 99 per cent might ignore the good result and concentrate on the one per cent that they got wrong.

You may also start jumping to negative conclusions and jumping to general conclusions from single events.

Depressive thinking

Depressive thinking makes a person see the world in a negative light. There are three elements to depressive thinking:

1. Negative thoughts, for example, 'I am a failure at work'

2. High, unreasonable expectations, for example, 'I cannot be happy unless everyone likes me and thinks I am good at my job'

3. Mistakes in thinking, for example:

    (a) jumping to negative conclusions
    (b) focusing on negative details of a situation and ignoring the good bits
    (c) coming to a general conclusion on the basis of a single incident
    (d) coming to the conclusion that things that are nothing to do with you are your fault

For instance, a fashion model I once treated thought that she was ugly and everyone hated her because a man who passed her in the street gave her a funny look.

These sorts of negative thinking patterns undermine you. They lead to worry, a lack of confidence and feelings of worthlessness, and your world becomes full of gloomy thoughts, self-doubt and anxieties. As a result, you feel more depressed or anxious and so a vicious circle is set up.

Case history: Carrie

Carrie is a secretary; her boss is late for the train and on his way out says, 'Could you type this report up for me, I have made a few corrections'. Carrie is depressed, and because of this she thinks she is a failure. She believes that she has to correct the report because she is bad at her job. She becomes more

depressed because she has the unreasonable expectation that she must be perfect in her job if she is to enjoy her life.

In reality, she is good at her job but she doesn't think so. She concentrates on little things that go wrong rather than the big things that go right. She forgets the fact that she was given a pay rise because her company value her so much. She also ignores the fact that her boss is known to be indecisive and always changes reports that he has written. She concentrates on the negative details and jumps to a general conclusion based on a single incident – this makes her depressed.

While she is typing the report another thought comes to her: 'Could the boss be late because he had to correct my sloppy work? If the deal falls through it will be all my fault!' She blames herself for things that are not her fault which fuels her depression.

Concentration and memory problems

If you are consumed by worries and depressive thoughts it can be difficult to think about anything else. You may find it difficult to concentrate and this leads to problems. You have to concentrate on something to remember it, so it is not surprising that poor concentration and memory problems go together. Problems with concentration also lead to indecision and inattention; you may feel muddled and confused. These can be so severe as to be mistaken for dementia.

Delusions and hallucinations
Delusions

If you should become severely depressed, your thinking can become so distorted that you lose touch with reality. Your mind can start playing tricks on you and you may even fear that you are going mad. You are not; you are severely depressed and will get better with treatment. Delusions can occur in severe depression; thankfully, they are rare (because they are so distressing).

A delusion is a false belief which is held unshakeably by the person who has it. In depression delusions reflect and reinforce the depressed mood as happened with James whom I treated some time ago. He believed that he should give himself up to the police because he had left a shop without paying for an apple by mistake five years previously. He thought that the police were looking for him and that there was no way out. He believed that he had brought shame on his family and was worthless. It was impossible to make him believe that he was not public enemy number one, that anyone could make a mistake and that no one would be bothered about it.

Other people believe that they are the most wicked person in the world or that people want to get rid of them because they are so bad. Some people believe that they have no money at all, others that they are decaying or even that they are dead. There are as many different types of delusion as there are ideas in the human mind but all of them reflect the depressed mood and depressive thinking.

Hallucinations

Whereas delusions are false thoughts, hallucinations involve perceiving things that are not real – usually sounds. For example, some severely depressed people hear voices when there is no one there. The voices sound like people in the room talking to them and are frighteningly real. The voices may criticise them or tell them that they are bad. The voices reinforce the depression. Some people see or smell things that are not there but this is rarer.

Suicidal impulses

When you are in the depths of depression the past looks bad and full of mistakes, the present is awful and you dread the future. Some come to the conclusion that life is not worth living, that everyone would be better off without them and that they should take their own life.

Many depressed people think about suicide – even if it is just a passing thought. Many do not actually contemplate committing suicide but go to bed at night hoping that they will not wake up, and so get away from the terrible torture of living.

Most people decide that they can't do it, perhaps because it would be too drastic, or the effect it would have on their family or because of religious beliefs. Some people come to the conclusion that they have not done it because they are cowards and this makes them feel even more ashamed and depressed.

If you think about suicide you are at risk of doing it. Get help urgently: see a GP, go to an accident and emergency department or call the Samaritans. Depression can be treated.

Physical symptoms

Depression can cause a number of physical symptoms. Those people affected often come to the conclusion that they have a physical illness because they feel so tired and off-colour or are in pain.

Sleep problems

Sleep problems are common in depression and are sometimes partially to blame for the tiredness that may

be experienced. If you are suffering from a moderate or severe depression you may wake up in the morning hours earlier than usual and then find it impossible to get back to sleep. All depressed people can find it difficult to get to sleep because they worry and may suffer from broken nights – waking up a number of times before the morning.

Mental and physical slowing

If you are depressed you may feel like a machine that is seizing up. You feel tired all the time, it is hard to perform everyday chores, everything is an effort and it seems as if everything is slowed down. Your speech may be slow and monotonous and you may even move slowly. Doctors call this psychomotor retardation.

Sometimes body functions slow down or seize up as well. You may find that you have a dry mouth or that you become constipated; some women stop having menstrual periods or they may become irregular.

Loss of appetite

When you are depressed you can lose quite a lot of weight. Food seems unappetising and bland and you don't even feel hungry. Some people with severe depression stop eating and drinking completely, but this is rare.

Reverse physical symptoms

Instead of the normal physical symptoms of depression such as poor sleep, loss of appetite and loss of weight, some people have what are known as reverse physical symptoms. They sleep more, have a bigger appetite and gain weight. If you feel low in mood and have these symptoms you should see your doctor.

Other physical symptoms

Depression can produce just about any physical symptom. Pain and a feeling of pressure are common, most often affecting the head, face, back, chest and gut. People frequently come to hospital accident and emergency departments complaining of chest pain and worried that something is wrong with their hearts, when in fact they are suffering from depression. The pain is real but is caused by depression; there is nothing wrong with their hearts.

Sex

Many people go off sex when they are depressed. There are many reasons for this. Some people do not feel able to fulfil a physically loving relationship when they are emotionally numb. Other people feel so negative about themselves that they cannot relax. These psychological problems can lead to physical problems: men may find it difficult to get an erection and women may find that they are dry and that intercourse is painful. Many people who are depressed cannot say why but just do not feel interested in sex.

'Smiling' depression

Not everyone with depression feels low – some people say that they do not feel depressed but go to their GP with bodily symptoms such as pain, headache or tiredness that point to depression. Physical examination and investigation do not reveal a physical cause for their illness and the only treatment that works is antidepressant medication. It may be that their subconscious mind is playing tricks on them and does not allow their conscious mind to admit that they feel depressed.

What causes the symptoms?
Chemical deficiences

The symptoms of depression may be caused by low levels of certain chemicals in the brain. To understand why this might be, we need to look at how the brain works. The brain is made up of billions of nerve cells. It can take hundreds of these nerve cells to carry out the smallest action, even to think about doing something. In order for nerve cells to work together they have to communicate with each other and they do this by releasing chemicals called neurotransmitters.

Between the end of one nerve cell and the next there is a small space called the synapse. The first nerve cell communicates with the next by releasing neurotransmitters into the synapse. These neurotransmitters attach to the next nerve cells and so pass on the message.

Studies have shown that three important neurotransmitters, dopamine, serotonin and noradrenaline, are in short supply in depression. The levels are low in synapses, and this leads to faulty brain communication and message passing which may be the cause of depressive symptoms.

Nobody knows what causes these low levels of chemicals. Scientists do not know whether:

- they cause the depressed mood
- they are caused by the depressed mood.

It may be that low levels of neurotransmitters are caused by stress and then they lead to depression. Antidepressant drugs work by increasing the levels of these neurotransmitter chemicals.

How nerve cells transmit signals

Essentially, your brain is like a bundle of telephone wires transmitting and receiving messages within your brain and to and from other parts of your body. Some of the messages are sent by electrical impulses; others depend on the release and transmission of particular chemicals called neurotransmitters.

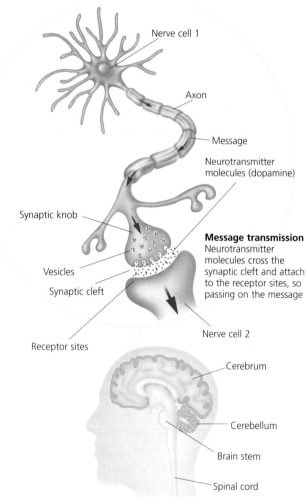

Nerve cell 1

Axon

Message

Neurotransmitter molecules (dopamine)

Synaptic knob

Message transmission
Neurotransmitter molecules cross the synaptic cleft and attach to the receptor sites, so passing on the message

Vesicles

Synaptic cleft

Nerve cell 2

Receptor sites

Cerebrum

Cerebellum

Brain stem

Spinal cord

The role of hormones

Hormones may be important in causing depression. The role of female hormones in depression is discussed on page 103. In this section I discuss the role of stress hormones. Depression is closely linked to stressful experiences.

Stress hormones

When you are stressed a complex series of hormones is released by your body: first your brain releases the hormone corticotrophin-releasing factor, which triggers the release of another brain hormone adrenocorti-cotrophic hormone (ACTH). ACTH travels in the bloodstream to your abdomen where it causes two small glands perched on top of your kidneys (the adrenal glands) to release cortisol.

Cortisol, corticotrophin-releasing factor and ACTH work together with adrenaline (epinephrine) to make you feel scared and anxious and get your body ready to deal with the source of the stress.

In most people hormone levels return to normal once the stressful situation has passed but in depression the system is hyperactive and cortisol levels do not follow the normal pattern.

In healthy people cortisol is usually released in large quantities in the morning and diminishing amounts throughout the day, whereas in some depressed people its release is the same all day long. Nobody knows whether this leads to depression or is the result of it, but cortisol is known to affect the levels of neurotransmitters in the brain.

Measurement of the changing levels of cortisol in the body has led to a test for depression, but it is not that sensitive and works only in about three in ten people. It works best in those who have serious depression with physical symptoms.

Brain cell death and growth

As our ability to investigate the brain has increased, we have developed better understanding of what is happening in depression.

Stress and depressed mood not only change the levels of hormones and neurotransmitters but also have subtle effects on the structure of the brain. They have temporary effects on the rate of death and birth of nerve cells. During bouts of depression some small areas of the brain seem to shrink and there are changes in the blood flow. Recent research has demonstrated that some antidepressants protect nerve cells from death, but it is not yet clear how important this is to how effectively they work.

KEY POINTS

- Depression has physical as well as mental symptoms

- Symptoms vary from person to person

- Anyone who thinks about suicide is at risk of doing it and should seek help urgently

Causes of depression

Why me, why now?

The questions most often asked by people who are depressed are 'Why me?' and 'Why now?'.

Sometimes there is an obvious cause for depression, such as bereavement, loss of a job or physical illness, but often there is not. To complicate the situation still further, depression doesn't affect everyone who is bereaved, loses their job or gets ill. We all have strengths and weaknesses. Some people may be more at risk of depression than others but, given the right circumstances, any of us could become depressed.

Researchers have a long way to go before they understand why people become depressed. Often there is more than one cause and having a problem that makes you prone to depression does not mean that you will develop it.

Factors that may make you prone to depression

Genes

Genes (the biological code that you inherit from your parents) are important in depression but there are many genes involved and no one knows exactly how they work. There is certainly no evidence of straightforward inheritance for most forms of depression.

You will not definitely develop depression because your mother, father, sister or brother has it, but your risk will be increased. You will be at highest risk if you have an identical twin who has developed depression.

It is difficult to put figures on this risk because the importance of genes is different for different types of depression. They are more important in severe than in mild depression and more important in young people who get depressed than in older people who get depressed. Genes are most important in the minority of people who have periods when their moods are high and periods when their moods are low – bipolar disorder or manic depression.

Even if there is depression in the family, there will usually need to be some sort of stressful life event to trigger it.

Personality

No single type of personality predisposes people to depression. However, those who are obsessional, dogmatic and rigid, and who hide their feelings may be more at risk, as may those who get anxious easily.

People who have repeated and sustained up and down moods are more likely to develop manic–depressive illness. However, the vast majority of people who have depression do not have any of these personality types.

Family environment
Losing a parent in childhood
There is some evidence that people who lose their mother when they are young have an increased risk of depression. Suffering that sort of loss might scar you psychologically and make you more susceptible to depression but, on the other hand, it might make you more resilient. It may be the psychological, social and financial consequences of losing a parent, rather than the loss itself, that are important.

Type of parenting

Psychologists claim that demanding, critical parents who take any success for granted but are harsh on any kind of failure may make their children more prone to depression in the future. Psychotherapists have suggested that people who have little maternal affection when they are young are at risk of depression in later life but there is no scientific proof for this.

Physical or sexual abuse in childhood

There is some evidence that physical or sexual abuse can make people prone to severe depression in later life. Studies have shown that up to half of the people who see a psychiatrist have had some kind of unwanted sexual attention during early adolescence or childhood.

People who have been abused generally remember the abuse but some people first remember childhood abuse when they are depressed and having psychotherapy. There is disagreement between specialists as to whether these memories are always real. Some argue that, on rare occasions, psychotherapists who believe that sexual abuse is the cause of their patient's problem can make the patients remember things that never actually happened by suggesting to them that they did. This is known as false memory syndrome.

Gender

Women are twice as likely to be diagnosed as being depressed as men. This does not necessarily mean that women are more prone to depression. It may be that women are more likely to admit to depression than men or that doctors are more likely to recognise it in women. There are, however, social pressures on

Factors that influence depression

Both long-standing factors and current difficulties may play a part in causing someone to become depressed.

Factors that may make you prone to depression:

- Genes
- Personality
- Family environment
- Gender
- Thinking patterns
- Having little control of your destiny
- Stress and life events
- Physical illness
- Lack of daylight

Factors that can trigger depression:

- Stress
- Physical illness
- Prescription medication
- Lack of daylight

women which lead to depression that men are less likely to encounter – like being alone at home with small children. There are also hormonal changes throughout the menstrual cycle and related to pregnancy and childbirth and to the menopause that may make women more prone to become depressed or to trigger a bout of depressive illness. (For more on this, see page 103.)

Thinking patterns

In 1967 an American psychiatrist, Aaron Beck, described patterns of thinking that are common in depression and that he thought made people prone to getting depression. In short, he believed that people who are very negative about themselves are prone to getting depression.

Most of us have an optimistic way of thinking which keeps us moderately cheerful most of the time. We tend to belittle our failures and make the most of our successes. For example, if you spill a drink in a crowded pub you may say the glasses were overfilled or someone pushed you – it was not your fault. However, if you get through the mass of people without spilling a drop you may be unlikely to say that the glasses were underfilled or everyone else was careful not to push you. You may claim it as a feat of skill.

Some people who are prone to depression think the other way around. They tend to belittle their successes and dwell on their failures. There is evidence that people think like this when they are depressed, but there is no good evidence that they think like this before they get depressed. The importance of this theory is that it has led to 'cognitive therapy', one of the most exciting new treatments of depression (see page 65).

Having little control over your destiny

Some specialists believe that people placed for a long time in a situation over which they have no power and from which they cannot escape are prone to develop depression.

The idea came from experiments with dogs performed by a psychologist. He found that they became demoralised and passive, and ate less if they were put in experimental conditions where they were given mild punishment for no apparent reason and consequently had no way of controlling it. He called this learned helplessness.

Other specialists believe that it is difficult to equate the actions of dogs with those of humans and it is very difficult to say whether dogs ever get depressed. However, rates of depression are high in those bed-bound or wheelchair-bound patients who rely on nurses for everything.

Long-term disabling illnesses

Discomfort, disability, dependency and insecurity can make it more likely that a person will become depressed. Most of us prefer to be independent and like to meet people. Being forced into a position where they are relatively helpless may be one way in which severely ill people become prone to depression or it may be that the energy needed to fight off depression is sapped by long-term illnesses. Worries over financial insecurity may also be important.

Factors that may trigger depression
Stress and life events

Stress can lead to depression whether it comes in the form of a sudden, overwhelming event or as long-term stress. Depression is six times more common in the six months after a markedly stressful life event. Stress can make you more prone to developing depression or can trigger it off.

Life events such as loss of a partner or loss of a job may be the final straw if you have long-term difficulties such as housing, marriage and/or work problems. The

Top 10 stressful life events

- Death of a spouse
- Divorce
- Marital separation
- Prison term
- Death of a close friend
- Injury or illness
- Marriage
- Losing your job
- Marital reconciliation
- Retirement

long-term problems magnify the effect of the short-term problem.

The experiences that trigger depression are usually losses of some kind – such as losing your job, the death of someone you love (see Grief and bereavement, page 123) or the loss of a partner through divorce. However, they may also be losses of a more subtle kind, such as loss of self-esteem through a destructive relationship.

Only one in ten of such 'loss events' leads to depression and other experiences in life that sometimes trigger depression do not involve loss of any kind. We all have our own psychological ways of reacting to stress and it is not possible to predict how we will react.

Physical illness

Physical illness can set off depression. The shock of finding out that you have a serious illness can lead to a loss of confidence and self-esteem, and so to depression.

Some illnesses linked with depression

- Acromegaly
- Addison's disease
- Alcohol: direct effect on the brain and also because it ruins your life
- Brain abscess
- Brain haemorrhage
- Brain tumours
- Chronic fatigue syndrome
- Cushing's disease
- Dementia
- Diabetes
- Encephalitis
- Head injuries
- Heart problems
- Hyperparathyroidism
- Hypopituitarism
- Hypothyroidism
- Multiple sclerosis
- Parkinson's disease
- Severe head injury
- Tuberculosis, meningitis
- Vitamin deficiency
- Viral illnesses (including flu and glandular fever)
- Water balance problems (such as low salt, high calcium or low calcium in your body)

But the reasons are complex: for instance, depression is quite common after a heart attack, possibly because people feel that they had a near miss and it makes them face their own mortality or perhaps because they become suddenly disabled. In older people physical illness is one of the most common causes of depression.

Some illnesses can cause depression because of the way that they affect the body. Depression can accompany Parkinson's disease and multiple sclerosis partly because of their effects on the brain. Illnesses that affect your hormones can cause depression.

There's also a link with viral illnesses: an epidemic of influenza is often followed by an epidemic of depression and many of us will know someone who has become depressed after a bout of glandular fever. How a virus causes depression is not clear, but one theory is that viruses use up the body's supplies of vitamins, so weakening it.

Prescription medicines

Some prescription medications can cause depression (see box), but you shouldn't stop taking any of the medicines on the list without con-sulting your doctor. These drugs do not always cause depression and it may be that you have another reason for being depressed. Sometimes stopping the medication that you are taking can be more dangerous than depression.

Some medicines that may cause depression

- Anti-epilepsy tablets
- Anti-high blood pressure drugs
- Anti-malarial drug – mefloquine (Lariam)
- Anti-parkinsonian drugs
- Chemotherapy drugs (some) used in the treatment of cancer
- Contraceptive pill (combined contraceptive pill and possibly reports in progestogen-only pill)
- Digitalis (heart)
- Diuretics (heart and blood pressure)
- Interferon-alfa used in the treatment of hepatitis C
- Major tranquillisers
- Steroid therapy (for asthma, arthritis, etc.)

Non-prescription medication can also lead to depression. Alcohol has direct effects on the brain and can make you feel depressed. Alcoholism can also cause depression because of the negative effect that it has on your life. Similarly recreational drugs can have an effect through direct effects and the impact that they have on your lifestyle.

Lack of daylight

Most of us feel better in the sun than on overcast days and prefer the summer to the winter, but this takes an extreme form in some individuals. They are fine in summer but become depressed as the days grow shorter at the onset of winter. They are said to suffer from seasonal affective disorder (SAD).

SAD may be related to the levels of a hormone called melatonin which is released from the pineal gland in the brain. Its release is sensitive to light; more is released when it is dark. Light therapy is sometimes very effective in getting rid of the symptoms of seasonal affective disorder. Four hours of bright light a day from a special lamp can lift depression within a week.

KEY POINTS

- There are many possible reasons for depression

- Some physical illnesses and some tablets cause depression

- Usually there are a number of causes for any person's depressive illness

Types of depression

Classifying depression

When you see a doctor, counsellor or other professional, you may hear a variety of terms used to describe your illness. Some have overlapping meanings, but in this book the terms mild, moderate and severe depression are used throughout, and these have clear distinguising characteristics.

Mild depression

In mild depression the low mood may come and go and the illness often starts after a specific stressful event. The person may feel anxious as well as feeling low. Lifestyle changes are often all that are needed to lift this kind of depression.

Moderate depression

In moderate depression low mood is persistent and the person has physical symptoms as well, although they will vary from person to person. Changes in lifestyle alone are unlikely to work and medical help is needed.

Severe depression

Severe depression is a life-threatening illness in which symptoms are intense. The person will experience physical symptoms, delusions and hallucinations, and it is important to see a doctor as soon as possible.

Other terms for depression

Other terms in common use among the medical professional to describe types of depression include the following.

Reactive depression

This term is used in two ways by doctors. In the first, reactive is used to describe a depression that is caused by a stressful event – such as losing your job – and doesn't usually last long. It could be described as a short-lived exaggeration of a normal response to adversity. Counselling, family support, stress management and practical steps may be all that are needed to treat it.

However, a stressful event can trigger more severe depression and people who are prone to depression can have stressful life events after their illness starts. If this happens it is difficult to pinpoint exactly whether the depression is truly a reaction to stress.

The term 'reactive' is also used to describe a depression in which a person can still react to and enjoy social situations.

Endogenous depression

Endogenous depression comes on for no reason; it is usually intense and the person is likely to have physical symptoms such as loss of appetite and weight, early morning wakening, mood worse in the morning and loss of interest in sex. It will usually get better only with treatment.

The trouble with using this particular way of defining depression is that the same symptoms can be triggered in some people by stressful events. Also, just because you can't put your finger on any particular stressful event that set the depression off, it doesn't mean that there wasn't one.

Neurotic depression

This term is used to describe a mild form of depression in which the person has good and bad days. They tend to feel more depressed in the evenings. With this kind of depression, you may well experience difficulty getting off to sleep and have interrupted sleep but no early morning wakening. Some people sleep excessively and some find that they are more irritable than usual. Neurotic can be used as a term of abuse so the description neurotic depression is not used much these days and, in any case, it is really just another name for mild depression.

Psychotic depression

Psychotic depression is severe and people who have it will experience physical symptoms and may lose touch with reality. They may have delusions and/or hallucinations. People with psychotic depression always need medical treatment.

Bipolar disorder

Bipolar disorder or depression is another name for manic–depressive illness. People with manic–depressive illness have sustained high moods and periods of sustained low moods which can range from mild to severe depression.

When people with this illness are in one of the high moods (manic), they are likely to feel elated, need less sleep or food than usual, and experience a general feeling of well-being. They have excessive amounts of energy, speak very quickly and feel as if thoughts are racing in their head. Their judgement is likely to be poor and they may also experience delusions and hallucinations but these are the opposite to those in depression – their content is much more positive. Some people believe that they know the Royal Family or are VIPs when they are not, others that they are rich or have special powers. High moods can be as destructive as low ones and sometimes the lack of sound judgement and delusions can lead to financial trouble as a result of impulse buying – perhaps a yacht or a wildly expensive house.

Unipolar depression
Unipolar depression is a term that is used to describe the kind of depression experienced by the vast majority of people and means that they have only low moods, not high ones as well.

Agitated depression
Agitated depression is actually a description of the symptoms of this type of depression, in which the individual is anxious, worried and restless.

Retarded depression
Retarded depression is again a description of symptoms and refers to the kind of depression in which both mental and physical processes are slowed down and the person often finds it difficult to concentrate. When the illness is very severe, some people find it impossible

to move, speak or eat and there is a risk that they might starve.

Dysthymia

This terms refers to mild depression that is persistent. Although it may come and go, doctors will make this diagnosis if the illness has gone on for more than two months in two years. The main symptoms are indecision and low self-esteem. Psychotherapy may work better than drug treatment.

Masked (smiling) depression

People with masked depression say they do not feel depressed even though they have a number of other symptoms that point to depression. They may be investigated for physical illnesses before the diagnosis is made. Symptoms, such as chest pain or sleep problems, get better when the person is given antidepressant treatment.

Organic depression

This is the name given to a kind of depression that is caused by a physical illness or medication.

Brief recurrent depression

This is a recently recognised illness in which serious depression comes on and lasts for only a few days at a time.

Seasonal affective disorder (SAD)

This term was originally used to mean any depressive illness that came on regularly at a certain time of year – say because of increased demands at work. It is now used for a specific type of depression that may result from decreasing levels of daylight as winter approaches and days get shorter. People with SAD may experience cravings for carbohydrate and/or chocolate, and an increased need for sleep.

KEY POINTS

- There are many types of depression

- Mild depression may not need drug treatment, but moderate and severe depression often do

- Depression may be constant or come and go

- Depression may be associated with other non-mood symptoms

Helping yourself

Involve your doctor

Many people with mild depression get better by using simple self-help measures alone. There are lots of examples of guided self-help plans that you can get from your GP or even on the internet.

Even if you decide that you are going to use self-help alone, it is still worth seeing your GP for a number of reasons, for instance your depression may be caused by a physical illness; also if a GP assesses you then at a later date he or she will be in a position to give you an independent view as to whether self-help has worked for you.

People with more severe forms of depression will also benefit from using self-help measures, but they should be used as part of a plan discussed with their doctor or therapist. Self-help measures may help to stave off depression as well as to treat it and promote recovery. Do not try to do everything at once – consider which of the suggestions could make a difference to you and then have a go. You will feel better for it.

Be prepared for difficulties

People often become depressed following a loss of some kind, but sometimes it may be possible to prepare yourself when you know that you are going to have to face up to a change. The kind of predictable things that can trigger depression include loss of social support when a person goes to university, loss of freedom or work status when a woman takes maternity leave, and loss of work routine and social contact for some people when they retire. Not surprisingly rates of depression are high at around these times.

There are two ways to decrease the stress of predictable losses:

(1) being open and acknowledging that there may be a problem

(2) by preparing for the change.

If you acknowledge your feelings you will feel better. If you are worried about the change in your life, talk it through with a friend – let other people know your concerns and they may be able to support you. Saying how you feel may change the way that they treat you: for example, if you are retiring, they may stop telling you that you should be happy at not having to work any more, they may spend more time with you or expect less of you while you're adjusting to your new situation.

Good preparation for any change is helpful; reading about it, or talking to people who have gone through a similar experience, will be useful. Taking common-sense measures to decrease the stress and trying to arrange in advance your first few days or weeks may help the transition.

For instance, if you are going to university, you may find that there are people you know there whom you could arrange to meet up with or you could practise cooking some simple meals before you go so you have one less problem to fret about. The early weeks of retirement can be planned so that there is social support and you have something to do. Many women find support groups, such as the National Childbirth Trust, invaluable after they have had a baby.

Take a break

If you are feeling down or you feel that everything is getting on top of you, take a break, even if you can manage only a day or a night away, but, better still, take a proper holiday if you can. It is not running away and you will get only a little behind in your work.

You will probably find that you may be able to think through your problems better if you are away from them and you may work much better when you get back. A break may give you the rest you need to attack your problems and the distance to put them in proper perspective. If you find that you cannot enjoy a few days away this is a sign that you need professional help.

Talk things over

You will find that, if you talk problems over with your partner, a friend or family member, you will feel better. It not only decreases the burden on you, but just talking through things may also help you find a solution.

You may discover that your friends have their own ideas about what you should do and may think of solutions that haven't occurred to you. They may have gone through the same kind of difficulties that you are experiencing and so be able to give you insights into your problems.

People often feel better after they have had a good cry. The open acknowledgement of your problems is often the starting point for working out solutions.

Many people who are depressed cut themselves off and think that they are a burden to other people. In fact, this just makes you more depressed so do try instead to choose a friend who will be sympathetic and willing to listen to you and help you through a difficult time. Everyone needs help at some time.

Change your lifestyle

See whether you can identify and change aspects of your life that may have brought on the depression.

You may need help to do this but it is not as impractical as it seems. Somebody else has usually gone through the same problem before and there may be a way in which you can solve it too. If you are worried about an illness you should discuss this with your doctor; things may not be as bad as they seem. If it is a social or legal problem you could visit a Citizens Advice Bureau for help.

Get in touch with a group

There are many ways in which other people can help and joining a group of some kind can be a real support. Some possibilities that you might consider are listed in the section starting on page 136. Your GP should have information about what is available in your area. If you need help urgently and do not want to see your GP then you can call the Samaritans. They offer telephone and face-to-face counselling. There are a number of other organisations that offer more specialised help – for example, if your relationship is the cause of your depression, you could contact Relate and a counsellor will see you with your partner or alone. If you need help with bereavement, CRUSE specialise in this. See the 'Useful information' section on page 136

Exercise

Exercise can boost your well-being too. It doesn't just make you feel better psychologically; it also gets you out of the house and makes you fitter. It does not have to be Lycra-style aerobics. Going for a good walk or a swim will do just as well. Active pastimes such as bowling are a good way of getting out and doing something. If you have not done any exercise for a while, you should be careful and start slowly.

When you have a low mood it is sometimes hard to be motivated to exercise. Getting involved in a structured and supervised exercise programme can be the best way to make sure that you do enough and not too much, and that you continue to do it. GP surgeries can often offer advice on this.

Can you eat yourself happy?

The importance of a balanced diet

Diet is an important element to keeping depression at bay. Although it is unlikely that you will be able to eat yourself happy, it is important to eat properly during a bout of depression and a regular balanced diet with all the essential vitamins that may keep you feeling well when the bout is over.

If you are suffering from depression, cutting out caffeine is a good idea because it can make you feel anxious, and eating large amounts of carbohydrates may produce swings in your mood and is best avoided.

What you eat may be more important in staving off depression than treating it when your mood is already low.

Food that may improve your mood

Selenium (oysters, mushrooms, Brazil nuts), zinc (shellfish, seafood, eggs) and chromium (green vegetables, poultry – especially turkey and dietary supplements from health food shops) can improve your mood, but they should not be taken in high doses

Some scientists have claimed that eating fish can help depression. This is because studies have shown that fish oils have antidepressant and mood-stabilising properties. Unfortunately, you would have to eat an awful lot of fish to get enough fish oil to make any difference. As a result of this some companies have started to produce capsules that contain concentrated fish oil. Apart from a slight upset stomach most people have no side effects. Unfortunately, their impact on mood is far from proven.

Can you eat yourself happy? (contd)

Vitamin B

Very large doses of vitamin B taken for a year may improve your general well-being according to one study. But beware because there have been reports of irreversible damage to the nerves if you take too much vitamin B_6.

The theory is based on the fact that some people with depression have low levels of folate in the blood. Folate is found in lots of foods including cereals, citrus fruit, lettuce, peanuts and chickpeas. But although low in depression, it is not clear whether eating folate-rich foods once you are depressed will lift your mood.

Eating a balanced diet rich in mood-enhancing foods and cutting out too much carbohydrate, caffeine and alcohol is generally good for you, whether or not it cures a bout of depression.

Look after yourself
Activities

If you are feeling depressed keeping occupied often helps. Taking up a new activity or hobby at an evening class or at the weekend is one idea. Getting out of the house and meeting people will do you good because it breaks the vicious circle of loneliness and spending too much time mulling over your problems.

Make a conscious effort to do what you like doing – listening to a CD, shopping, having a massage, going to a concert or a film. Little things can make a big difference.

Food and nutrition

Even if you do not have much of an appetite make
sure that you eat regularly and if you cannot face a
meal go for balanced snacks instead. If you do not eat
properly you will not have the physical strength to get
better and you will start descending into the vicious
circle of worse and worse depression. If you really cannot
face eating properly, or preparing a meal, soluble
powders, such as Complan, can be bought from
pharmacies without a prescription. They contain a whole
day's nourishment in a liquid form and are easy to
prepare.

Alcohol

Remember that alcohol will not sort out your
problems. It will make you feel more depressed and
could become a habit that ruins your life. Alcohol

Alcohol will not sort out your problems.

decreases inhibitions and may lead to suicidal impulses taking over. You should also be careful about drinking alcohol if you are taking antidepressants.

Sleep

Sleeping problems are common and depressed people are especially prone to insomnia. Lack of sleep makes it more difficult to summon up the energy to fight depression.

If your depression is moderate or severe, self-help may not be enough and you may need medication to sort out your insomnia.

Stress management
Relaxation

This is easier said than done and is something that we all need help with but there are many ways of relieving tension and one of them will work for you. One thing that many relaxation techniques have in common is that they teach you to recognise when your muscles are tense and how to relieve the tension. You can learn this by going to a relaxation group, by buying relaxation tapes or by reading about it. Your GP may have a relaxation group or relaxation trainer at the surgery. This is often a good place to start and after a couple of sessions you will probably be able to do it yourself.

There are more elaborate methods of relaxation such as meditation and fancy sounding ways of teaching you to know when you are tense such as bio-feedback.

Biofeedback relaxation

This is aided by a machine that monitors either muscle responses or electrical activity in the skin. When you

How to get a good night's sleep

Prolonged bouts of insomnia can be very stressful and will make your depression much more difficult to cope with. Listed below are some useful tips to help you get a good night's sleep.

- Get up earlier in the morning to see if this helps
- Take some exercise during the day
- Do not take naps
- Do not exercise just before bed – it can make it difficult to sleep
- Do not have a heavy meal late at night; you could feel uncomfortable – but do not go to bed hungry
- Do not drink coffee, tea or cola in the evening
- Have a milky warm drink last thing before going to bed
- Get your mind off your problems by reading a book before trying to sleep
- Go to bed at a regular time so that your body sets up a natural rhythm
- Do not drink alcohol to help you sleep – it may not work and you may not be able to break the habit
- Make sure that your bed is comfortable
- Make sure that the room is not too hot or too cold
- Do not smoke before you go to sleep – nicotine is a stimulant and there is a danger of fire
- Sexual intercourse before you go to sleep can help you wind down
- Do relaxation exercises before you go to bed
- Remember – if you can't get off to sleep for half an hour or if you wake up at night and can't get back to sleep, get up and read a book or watch TV. Lying there worrying will not do you any good – it could make things worse!

are more tense electrical activity in the skin and muscle increases and this causes the machine to produce a signal – either a high-pitched whistle or a light coming on. When you relax the sound gets lower in frequency or the light goes off – so you learn how to relax your muscles.

Autogenic training

This is a series of simple mental exercises in which the patient is encouraged to enter a state of passive concentration – it is a form of meditation that can reduce stress and make people more relaxed.

You will usually need professional help for these exercises, and many of the techniques involved in autogenic training are no more effective than simple relaxation training.

Massage

This can be done by yourself, your partner or a professional. There are plenty of devices that can be bought to help you massage yourself, but it is usually best to get someone else to do it. You may be able to talk over your problems at the same time. Specialist types of massage, Shiatsu, reflexology and aroma-therapy, are all good for stress.

Shiatsu

This is a Japanese massage technique built on traditional Chinese medical theory. Our vital life force or Qi is believed to flow through our bodies in certain pathways or meridians. If it gets blocked or there is an imbalance it leads to disease. In Shiatsu massage pressure points are manipulated to unblock or balance Qi.

Relaxation exercise

This is a simple method for relaxing. It only takes 20 minutes maximum. You can do it in bed, lying on the floor or sitting in a comfortable chair. Just make sure that any chair you use supports your neck. You may want to try it in the evening first time around – some people feel so relaxed that they fall asleep. Once you've got the hang of it you will be able to do it anywhere without dropping off, unless you want to.

1. Let your whole body
   go limp. Try to feel as
   heavy on the bed or
   in the chair as
   possible. Let the bed
   or the chair take your
   weight. Feel heavy,
   like a sack of
   potatoes.

2. Put your arms by your side and let them flop down. Let your legs go all floppy as well. Let your shoulders drop. Relax all parts of your body from the top down. Feel heavy on the bed or chair.

3. If you have not done relaxation exercises before, you will need t
   teach yourself how to relax your muscles. Tense the muscle in
   your upper leg harder and harder until you can't do it any more
   Now release it. You will feel the difference between tension

Relaxation exercise (contd)

and relaxation. Do the same from the top of your body to your toes. Start with your face – screw your face up, clench your teeth and then release.
Then make your neck muscles tense, then release. Shrug your shoulders so that they nearly touch your ears, then let them drop. Tense and release your arms, chest, stomach, backside, legs, feet and toes, one by one.

4. You will find that your muscles feel less tense than they did when you started. Remember what they feel like. Once you have the hang of it you will not need to tense your muscles before you relax them.

5. When you feel relaxed and limp, slow your breathing down bit by bit, making it slow and even. Concentrate only on your breathing. Make inhaling and exhaling the same length, long and slow. Stop if you feel light-headed. After 20 minutes you will feel much better than when you started. You will feel much calmer and more rested.

Reflexology

This is another ancient art of massage. Different areas on the foot are thought to be linked to certain body systems. Manipulation and massage of these areas are thought to put right problems that you have in the particular body system.

Aromatherapy

This uses the scents of plant oils and essential oils to aid psychological well-being.

Pet therapy

Some people who are prone to recurrent depressions find that it is therapeutic to get a dog or a cat. They are cuddly, reliable and responsive and may decrease your stress level. However, being given a pet when you are depressed will not necessarily make you better. Apart from the fact that a pet requires a lot of time and effort, it takes time to build up a relationship.

Complementary medicine
Homoeopathy

Homoeopathy is a form of medicine built on the principle that like heals like but that very small quantities of a substance can promote healing. For instance, a nettle extract may be prescribed for a skin rash, but this nettle extract will be so dilute that very little in the way of nettle remains. Despite this the nettle extract is thought to promote the body's own immune system. Before you consider going to see a homoeopath of your own accord, talk it over with your doctor first. Some GPs are trained homoeopaths and there are homoeopathic NHS hospitals. Your doctor can also give an opinion as to whether going to a homoeopath with your particular depression is a good idea and may know a good local practitioner.

Acupuncture

Acupuncture works on the same principles of Qi as Shiatsu; however, fine needles are inserted to points on the meridians to help balance Qi rather than massage. This is increasingly being used in the UK. There are a number of doctors who are trained in acupuncture as well as conventional western medicine. Its use in depression is still a matter for debate.

Chinese herbal medicine

Chinese herbalists have been treating common problems such as depression for centuries. It is unclear how effective their remedies are in the UK. If you decide to see one or take a prescription make sure that you tell your GP or psychiatrist. Some herbal cures interact with other drugs that your GP may give you.

Hypnosis

This can be used to aid relaxation but is not a treatment for depression. In hypnosis you enter a trance, you are not asleep and the hypnotist attempts to help you manipulate your subconscious mind. Some types of hypnosis have been used to stop people feeling anxious but there is little good evidence for them working in depression.

KEY POINTS

■ Self-help can be used as part of a plan agreed with your GP

■ Do not try to change everything at one time

■ Once you are well, self-help techniques may stave off depression in the future

Treatment

Talking to your doctor

If self-help does not work, or if your depression is severe
from the outset you should see your GP. He or she:

- is knowledgeable about depression

- will listen to you

- may know you and know your medical history

- can make sure that there are no physical problems
  that are causing the depression

- can arrange investigations or start treatment
- will be there to offer you support
- can sign you off work sick if need be
- can refer you to a specialist
- will know of other therapies available in your area.

Your GP should be the first port of call if you need help; however, if there is an emergency you can call the Samaritans or visit your local accident and emergency department. There, you will be assessed by a doctor and a psychiatrist can be called if necessary. In some areas hospitals have emergency psychiatric clinics that you can just walk into; in other areas there is a crisis intervention team who will see you at home.

Each of these services is used to dealing with people who are depressed and will offer high-quality treatment. No one will think that your problems are trivial or stupid. They will be eager to help – that is what they are there for.

Types of treatment

There are three types of treatment for depression:

(1) psychological treatments

(2) drug treatment (see page 70)

(3) physical treatments (see page 93).

The first two may be available through your GP; the last is available only from specialists and used only in very severe depression. Psychological treatments are dealt with in this chapter and medication and physical treatments in the next two.

Psychological therapies – talking therapies

Psychological therapies are the most popular type of treatment for depression, partly because they do not involve taking tablets and partly because they make intuitive sense. It seems right to sit down and talk about things if they are getting on top of us. It also seems right to try to get to the bottom of why we feel the way we do when depression comes on for no reason.

However, you may be too depressed to be able to think clearly and may be too tired to start psychotherapy. All psychological therapies take a lot of time and commitment. They are not an easy option. They take a lot of energy. If your depression is severe, you may need to lift your depression with antidepressant medication before you consider psychological treatment. You should see your doctor to discuss what is available in your area.

There are many different types of psychological therapy and they are based on different theories.

Treating different types of depression

Depending on whether your GP or another specialist judges your depression to be mild, moderate or severe, different kinds of treatment will be recommended.

Mild depression

Self-help, lifestyle changes and psychotherapy often work. Medication will often be prescribed only if self-help, exercise and forms of psychotherapy have not worked. Medication is not as effective in mild depression and the side effects can outweigh the beneficial effects.

Moderate depression

Either medication or specific forms of psychotherapy can work here depending on your symptoms. Some doctors believe that a combination of both is required. If you have early morning wakening, depression worse in the morning, loss of appetite or weight, and loss of interest in things that you used to enjoy, antidepressants will work and work well. However, cognitive–behavioural and interpersonal therapy also work well in moderate depression and, if they are available and you would prefer not to take medication, you could try these types of therapy first. See your doctor regularly so that you can be monitored. If things get worse you should reconsider starting medication.

Treating different types of depression (contd)

Severe depression
Many people with severe depression are too ill to benefit from psychotherapy and need to start taking antidepressants. People who are actively suicidal need urgent help and to be in a safe place.

If the depression is characterised by delusions and hallucinations, an antidepressant may need to be combined with a special drug, an anti-psychotic, which will specifically treat these.

Recurrent depression
If you have been depressed before you should use the treatment that worked last time because it will do so again. Once you are well you should discuss long-term treatment with your doctor – lithium or a low dose of antidepressant can help stave off another attack.

Bipolar disorder or manic–depressive illness
Depression can be treated with antidepressants but your doctor will want to monitor your treatment carefully because, in a few people with up and down moods, antidepressants can lead to a high mood. In the long term other medications that act as mood stabilisers – such as lithium – may be more suitable.

They are most easily split into:

- brief therapies that last at most six months
- long-term therapies that last longer
- counselling.

Brief therapies usually consist of 4 to 20 weekly sessions, each lasting up to an hour. In long-term therapies there are usually over 50 sessions; they are often weekly but they can be five times a week. Brief therapies usually deal with problems in the here and now, whereas long-term therapies delve into the past to try to discover why you are the way that you are.

Counselling lasts for a variable time, from one session onwards. It does not aim to change deep-rooted problems or treat your depression, but it may help get rid of some of the problems that are causing you to be depressed.

Brief therapies

Many brief therapies are available on the NHS and your GP or a psychiatrist may suggest that you try one of these. The possibilities include:

- cognitive therapy
- cognitive analytical therapy
- cognitive–behavioural therapy
- behavioural therapy
- interpersonal therapy.

All of these have been used in depression.

Which kind of therapy you are offered may depend on what is available locally. Getting a good therapist is important, but the type of therapy that you get is also important. Many specialists currently favour cognitive–behavioural therapy and interpersonal therapy (see pages 66 and 67) over other brief therapies. Studies suggest that they can be as good as antidepressant treatment for treating bouts of moderate depression and decrease the risk of a relapse. Your therapist may be a doctor, a nurse, a psychologist, an occupational therapist or a social worker. If you have NHS psychotherapy it is likely that it will be supervised by a consultant psychotherapist to make sure that things go well.

There has been little guidance on how long a course of brief therapy should last. However, many of the studies that show benefit in depression use 16 to 20 sessions of therapy over a 6- to 9-month period. Following this, some also offer 2 to 4 top-up sessions over the next 6 to 12 months.

Cognitive therapy

Cognitive therapy works specifically on depressive thinking patterns. You will be asked to record your negative thoughts and look at the way that you think. You will then be helped to challenge thoughts that are unrealistically negative. Over 10 to 20 weekly sessions, the therapist tries to help you to stop thinking in a depressed way. This has been shown to work in even moderately severe depression. It can have benefits that last longer than medication alone. It can be used in combination with antidepressants. You should consider it seriously.

For instance our secretary Carrie from page 10 would be asked to work through her belief that she is a failure and present evidence for and against it. She would be helped to see that there are other ways of looking at the problem and that she does not have to be so hard on herself. She would be helped to think in a more balanced way. Perhaps she is not the best secretary in the world but she is a good secretary and even good secretaries make mistakes from time to time.

Behaviour therapy

This differs from cognitive therapy in that it focuses on what we do rather than what we think. Rather than trying to make you think less depressed, it makes you act less depressed. A behaviour modification programme may attempt to get you sleeping well, looking after yourself better and eating better. It stops you 'giving up'. Some people find this a first step back to recovery.

In Carrie's case all of these may be employed to make sure that she does not slip into a more severe depression. She would be encouraged to look after herself, have good sleep and eating habits, and make sure that she does not get into a depressive downward spiral.

Cognitive–behavioural therapy

This combines elements of cognitive therapy and behavioural therapy. It can be a potent treatment of mild and moderate depression. Trials have shown that it can be as effective as antidepressant drugs. It has been shown to get you better and keep you better. It can be used alone, but some studies have shown that the combination of cognitive–behavioural therapy and antidepressants is better than either alone.

Cognitive analytical therapy

This is another new therapy. It uses cognitive and behavioural techniques but also looks into your past to give you an idea where your ways of thinking come from. It is one of the few brief therapies that looks into the past and gives reasons for your problems.

If Carrie talked about her past it may have become clear that her parents were very critical. Her feelings of inferiority may have come from the way that she was undermined as a child. If she realised that the way she felt was because of circumstances and her childhood she may find it easier to accept herself for what she is and be less self-critical, dissatisfied and depressed.

Interpersonal therapy

Interpersonal therapy focuses on people's relationships and on problems such as difficulties in communication or coping with bereavement. Some consider it as effective as cognitive–behavioural therapy. An adequate course of interpersonal therapy is 16 to 20 sessions over a 6-month period.

Computerised therapies

A number of psychological therapies have been computerised, for instance it is possible to receive cognitive–behavioural therapy using a computer program rather than a therapist. Perhaps surprisingly to some, there are some reports that computerised cognitive–behavioural therapy is effective but more research is needed before it is accepted and widely available.

Long-term therapy

There are many different types of long-term therapy, all based on different theories. They may be available on the NHS, but there are usually long waiting lists. Long-term therapies try to deal with the deep-rooted causes of depression. They are not a quick treatment. Their aim is to sort out long-standing problems and they may not make you feel any less depressed in the short term.

Psychoanalysis

Psychoanalysts believe that our difficulties are caused by problems from the past that we have not dealt with. We may have denied them, ignored them or tried to forget them, but they are still in the backs of our minds. They stay there and fester and come back to us when we are under stress or weakened in some way. They can also weaken us. Such a problem could be the loss of a parent(s) when young at which time there was no proper grieving process and feelings were just covered up.

Long-term psychotherapy is said to work by helping these bad feelings come to the surface and into the consciousness. The aim is to disarm them and to stop them causing problems.

If you are thinking of having this sort of therapy, you should discuss it with your friends and your GP. There is a bewildering choice of people who offer psychotherapy and some poorly trained practitioners.

Counselling

Counsellors try to help you solve problems. They will not give advice but will help you to make decisions. Many counsellors are trained but some are not so it is a good idea to ask your GP for a recommendation or you may find that your local practice has a counsellor on site.

Couples therapy

Couples therapy is sometimes considered for those who are depressed, have a regular partner and who have benefited from brief individual therapy. There are many different types of couples therapy. They help couples to discuss their feelings and problems, to work out whether there is anything that they can do as a couple to improve the depression and to increase both partners' understanding of what is going on. Couples therapy lasts for 10 to 20 sessions over a 6-month period.

KEY POINTS

- Your GP should be the first port of call when you need help

- Some brief talking therapies have been shown to work well in depression

- Long-term psychotherapy tries to sort out problems that underlie the depression; it may not lift your depression in the short term

Medication

What is antidepressant medication?

Antidepressant tablets can be a very effective treatment for depression. When they are taken as prescribed and the recommended dosage is given, they often start to improve symptoms in two weeks, though it may take six weeks or more for the full benefit to be felt. You normally continue taking them for at least six months after the depression has vanished to make sure that it does not return, and then gradually stop.

Many doctors aim for someone who has had only one bout of depression to stay on medication for one year and for people who have had many episodes to stay on the medication for at least two years. Some recommend longer periods on antidepressants for older people. They work best for moderate and severe depression.

Will I become addicted?

Many people think they will become addicted to or dependent on antidepressants but this will not happen. Antidepressants are not like Valium (diazepam) and are not addictive. They work only if you are depressed and will not work if you are not. They do not give you a high. There is a black market trade in nearly all drugs that give you a high and can be addictive – there is no black market trade in antidepressants.

However, antidepressants are powerful drugs and some people who stop them suddenly feel peculiar. This is not a sign that you are dependent on or addicted to antidepressants; people who are addicted crave the drug to which they are addicted; people do not crave antidepressants and it is just that the body is used to having them around. Once you have recovered from depression, a gradual reduction in dose in the weeks before stopping will ensure that your body resets itself and that there are no symptoms.

How do antidepressants work?

In depression there are physical changes to the way in which your body works and antidepressants can put things back to normal. As we saw earlier (page 17), nerve cells in the brain are separated by a small space – the synapse. In order to pass messages to each other, nerve cells release chemicals (neurotransmitters) which leave one nerve cell and cross the space to the next nerve cell – like a baton in a relay race. The message is passed on only if there is enough neurotransmitter in the synapse. After release the neurotransmitters are broken up or taken back into the brain cell that released them.

The levels of these neurotransmitters are low in depression – it's as if the baton were being dropped. Antidepressants work by increasing the amount of neurotransmitters in the space between the cells – they put the baton back into the hand of the nerve cell.

The amount of neurotransmitter in the synapse can be increased by various drugs which work in different ways:

- Increasing the amount of neurotransmitter made (tryptophan).

- Preventing neurotransmitters being broken down (monoamine oxidase inhibitors or MAOIs).

- Stopping neurotransmitters in the synapse being taken back up into the cells (tricyclics, SSRIs, tricyclic-like compounds).

Over time the body rights itself, the amounts of neurotransmitters naturally produced increase and antidepressants are no longer needed.

Who needs antidepressants?

If you are mildly depressed you probably don't need this kind of treatment; with moderate depression you probably do and, with severe depression, you definitely do.

Medication should be prescribed after a full consultation with your GP or a psychiatrist as part of an agreed plan which might also include self-help techniques and psychotherapy. If you are having drug treatment this should be discussed with the therapist. If you are hesitant about taking antidepressants, remember that doctors do not prescribe anti-depressants to fob patients off. You may find it impossible to work through your problems unless you take them.

Certain symptoms – early morning wakening, depression that is worse in the morning, loss of appetite and weight, and loss of interest in things that you used to enjoy – indicate that your depression is very likely to respond to antidepressants.

The medication may have side effects. These are at their worst when you start treatment but get better as your body gets used to the drug. They can be reduced by starting at a low dose and building up or changing the drug that you are on. Most side effects are less of a bother than the depression. If the drugs are taken properly your depression will improve.

Antidepressants work best if you take a full dose. Low doses are not as effective and you may end up with side effects but no benefit. Try to persevere.

There are many different antidepressants available. They all work. Some are better for one type of depression than another and different kinds have different side effects.

After one episode of depression you will be advised to stay on medication for six months to make sure that the depression does not return. If you have had a previous bout of depression you may be advised to stay on medication for longer. Some doctors now advise their patients to stay on medication indefinitely if they have their first bout of depression after the age of 50, because there is a significant risk of a further bout.

Different types of antidepressants
Tricyclic antidepressants

These chemicals are called tricyclics because of their chemical structure – three rings that are linked together, with a side chain (like a tricycle). They increase the amount of neurotransmitter moving between brain cells by preventing it from being reabsorbed by the cell that released it. They are very effective in moderate or severe depression in which there are problems with sleeping, appetite, agitation or retardation. They take up to two weeks to start working.

How antidepressants are thought to treat depression

In depression, the levels of neurotransmitters are low.
Antidepressant drugs work to increase levels in one of three ways.

Depressed state (before treatment)

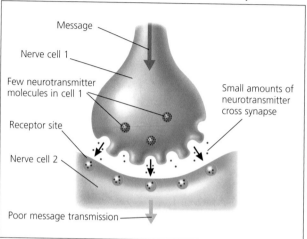

Message

Nerve cell 1

Few neurotransmitter
molecules in cell 1

Small amounts of
neurotransmitter
cross synapse

Receptor site

Nerve cell 2

Poor message transmission

1. Increasing amount of neurotransmitter

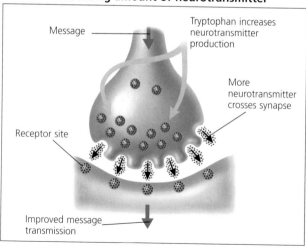

Message

Tryptophan increases
neurotransmitter
production

More
neurotransmitter
crosses synapse

Receptor site

Improved message
transmission

How antidepressants are thought to treat depression (contd)

2. Stopping breakdown of neurotransmitter

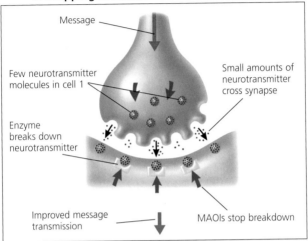

Message

Few neurotransmitter molecules in cell 1

Small amounts of neurotransmitter cross synapse

Enzyme breaks down neurotransmitter

Improved message transmission

MAOIs stop breakdown

3. Inhibiting reabsorption of neurotransmitter

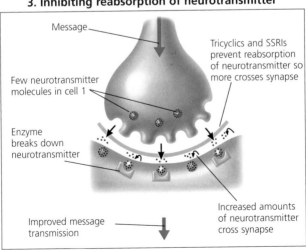

Message

Tricyclics and SSRIs prevent reabsorption of neurotransmitter so more crosses synapse

Few neurotransmitter molecules in cell 1

Enzyme breaks down neurotransmitter

Improved message transmission

Increased amounts of neurotransmitter cross synapse

Tricyclic antidepressants

Sedative tricyclics:
- Amitriptyline
- Clomipramine
- Dothiepin
- Doxepin
- Trimipramine

Non-sedative tricyclics:
- Amoxapine
- Desipramine
- Imipramine
- Lofepramine
- Nortriptyline

Stimulant tricyclic:
- Protriptyline

There are many different tricyclic antidepressants. They all work on depression but have other effects too. Some are sedatives – they calm you down – others are not.

If you are anxious and agitated your doctor will probably prescribe you a sedative antidepressant whereas if you feel slow and tired all the time your doctor will probably opt for one that is less sedating. Some people taking sedative tricyclics feel drowsy during the day. This can be reduced by taking the whole day's dose at night rather than three times a day. This may also make you sleep better.

If you drive for a living or use machinery, you should take special care when taking antidepressants. Discuss this with your doctor.

Tricyclics are powerful drugs and like all powerful drugs can have side effects, but some of the newer ones, such as lofepramine, have relatively few. Not everyone gets side effects but if you do tell your doctor. They can be reduced by starting the medication at a low level and building up the dose. They can also be reduced by changing the tricyclic that you take.

Some side effects of tricyclics

- Blurring of vision
- Constipation
- Difficulty getting an erection and in ejaculation
- Difficulty passing water
- Dry mouth
- Effects on the heart (makes it beat fast or irregularly)
- Fits are rare and occur only in people who are prone to them
- Giddiness on standing
- Sweating
- Tremor of the hands
- Weight gain

These antidepressants can interfere with other tablets that you take – even hay fever tablets that you buy over the counter – so you should consult your doctor and pharmacist before taking anything else.

An overdose of tricyclics can be fatal. There should be only a small number of these pills in the house if someone is suicidal.

Tricyclic-like antidepressants

There are many drugs that act just like tricyclics but do not have the three-ring structure and therefore aren't called tricyclics.

- Maprotiline has four rings. It should not be taken if you have had epilepsy.

- Mianserin has few side effects apart from an effect on the bone marrow which has led to it not being used very often.

- Iprindole can, very rarely, cause liver problems.

- Trazodone has few side effects, although, in men, it can rarely cause an erection that does not go away; this is quite painful.

- Viloxazine has fewer side effects than most tricyclics.

- Mirtazapine is an effective antidepressant that can cause blood disorders. Patients should consult their doctor if they have a fever or sore throat or any sign of infection while taking it. It can also increase your appetite and cause weight gain.

Selective serotonin re-uptake inhibitors (SSRIs)

These work in the same way as tricyclics – they stop neurotransmitters being taken back up into the cell that released them. However, they work on only one type of neurotransmitter – serotonin.

They are effective antidepressants. Initially they were thought to have fewer side effects than tricyclic antidepressants but now it is clear that they just have different side effects. They are less sedative, do not cause weight gain and do not affect the heart as much as tricyclics. As with tricyclics, caution is necessary in epilepsy and they can cause stomach problems initially. Diarrhoea, nausea and vomiting can occur as can headache, restlessness and anxiety. These drugs are much safer than tricyclics if they are taken as an overdose.

SSRIs have not been around as long as tricyclics. Many specialists believe that they are no better than tricyclics and, as they are very expensive, will

Some SSRIs

Real (generic) name	Trade (proprietary) name
Fluoxetine	Prozac
Fluvoxamine	Faverin
Paroxetine	Seroxat
Sertraline	Lustral
Citalopram	Cipramil

prescribe them only for people who can't take a tricyclic. But research seems to show that people who are on SSRIs are less likely to stop their medication because of side effects than those who take tricyclic antidepressants, so other authorities recommend SSRIs.

There has been much media hype about one drug – Prozac. This is an SSRI that works very much like the others, but has been popularised in some best-selling books. It has been called the 'happy pill' because it has the reputation of making people with mild depression happier. It has been prescribed to people with mild depression who probably may have got better with lifestyle changes alone. Currently in the USA there are many doctors worried about what they see as the over-prescription of this drug. Other SSRIs have similar functions and are as efficacious as Prozac.

Some side effects of SSRIs

- Stomach problems
- Diarrhoea
- Nausea
- Vomiting
- Headache
- Restlessness
- Anxiety

Some scientists have claimed that SSRIs cause suicidal and homicidal urges in some people. More work needs to be done on this subject but best advice is for anyone who thinks that they have this rare side effect to discuss it with their doctor.

Monoamine oxidase inhibitors (MAOIs)

These were the first antidepressants to be developed. They increase the amount of neurotransmitters in the synapse by stopping them being broken down by a substance called monoamine oxidase. Unfortunately, they also work in the rest of the body where monoamine oxidase has some important functions. One is to break down a chemical called tyramine which is in a number of foods. Too much tyramine causes high blood pressure and a violent throbbing headache and can lead to a stroke. As a result anyone who is taking these drugs must stick to a strict tyramine-low diet and carry a card with him or her.

It takes two weeks for the body to make new monoamine oxidase and so it takes two weeks for your body to get back to normal after you have stopped taking monoamine oxidase inhibitors. As a result of this you have to stay on the diet for this time; if they have not worked, you may not be able to try another antidepressant drug for this time.

Monoamine oxidase inhibitors (MAOIs)

MAOI
- Phenelzine
- Isocarboxazid
- Tranylcypromine

RIMA
- Moclobemide

There is a newer type of MAOI called a RIMA – reversible inhibitor of monoamine oxidase subtype A. There are two types of monoamine oxidase – type A and type B. As RIMAs inhibit only one type, there is less of a problem with tyramine-containing food, so the diet is less strict. However, people taking them do have to keep to the diet and could be at the same risk of problems if they eat too many tyramine-rich foods. RIMAs block the action of monoamine oxidase but do not destroy it, so the body does not have to make new monoamine oxidase and the effects are 'reversible' and wear off a day after stopping the drug.

MAOIs are used if a tricyclic or an SSRI has not worked, but some doctors use them from the start in depression with reverse physical symptoms (for example, where someone eats too much or sleeps more than usual) and they may also be used in people who have depressions that do not fit into any of the well-recognised patterns.

Other antidepressants
L-Tryptophan
This is thought to work by increasing the amount of neurotransmitter made by the brain cells. It is a chemical found in the diet which is turned into serotonin. It is a weak antidepressant but can be used in conjunction with other antidepressants.

Flupenthixol
This drug is used for other psychiatric illnesses but is a good antidepressant when given in low doses. It is relatively safe when taken as an overdose and has fewer side effects. If it is used for a long time, there can be serious side effects and it should be used only short term.

Nefazodone

This works as an SSRI but has fewer side effects on the stomach. It is better at helping sleep than most SSRIs.

Venlafaxine

This is an antidepressant that works like an SSRI. It can cause a skin rash and this should be reported to a doctor immediately because it may indicate a serious allergic reaction. Like many antidepressants, it may affect the performance of skilled tasks such as driving.

Reboxetine

This drug selectively inhibits the uptake of one neurotransmitter, noradrenaline.

Liothyronine

This is a hormone used in the treatment of people whose thyroid gland is underactive. In specialist centres, it may be used in conjunction with other treatments for people with severe depression.

Duloxetine

This is a new antidepressant that works both as an SSRI and similar to reboxetine in inhibiting the uptake of noradrenaline (norepinephrine). The makers hope that its two-pronged attack on depression will make it more effective.

St John's wort

Hypericum perforatum (St John's wort) is a popular herbal remedy for depression. You can buy it without a prescription. Many people who use it swear by it as their treatment of choice, especially in milder depression.

It is quite a powerful herb and can interact with other drugs that you are taking for physical conditions. If you are taking other medication, it is safest to tell your doctor before you start it and when you stop it. The amount of active ingredient in different preparations varies, so it is best to stick to one brand. If you are taking prescribed medications, different brands may interfere with them to different degrees.

Antidepressants and sex
Many people, when they are depressed, do not feel like having sex. This is part of the depression. However, problems with becoming aroused and ejaculation can also be a side effect of some antidepressant medications. If you are having any such problems you should speak to your doctor. Many people who are depressed suffer in silence, but GPs are aware of the side effect and it may be treated by changing the tablet that you are taking.

Mood stabilisers
These drugs are rarely used to treat depression; they are used to prevent it from coming back if you are prone to it by keeping your moods stable.

Lithium
Lithium makes our cells and our moods more stable. People who have bipolar disorder (manic–depressive illness) are less prone to breakdowns if they take lithium. It also prevents depression in people who suffer severe recurrent depression. It can stop relapses altogether or make them shorter and less severe with longer intervals between them.

Stopping antidepressants

Antidepressants should not be stopped without taking professional advice because withdrawal symptoms may occur.

General words of advice

- Do not stop antidepressants suddenly – they must gradually be tailed off over at least a month; consult your doctor first.
- Some people who have taken antidepressants regularly for weeks and stop suddenly suffer withdrawal symptoms.
- Withdrawal symptoms can be avoided if the dose of antidepressant is gradually reduced over at least four weeks.

Discontinuation symptoms

- Dizziness, electric shock sensations, anxiety and agitation, insomnia, flu-like symptoms, diarrhoea, nausea, abdominal pain, tingling of the fingers, mood swings, low mood.

Changing antidepressants

This should be done by a doctor. Some antidepressants should not be taken at the same time – they are potentially lethal in combination. You have to let all of one antidepressant leave your system completely before you start another one – this may take between one and five weeks, depending on which antidepressant you are stopping and which you are starting.

It has to be taken regularly and has to be at the right level in the blood. Too little does not work and too much causes side effects and can be life threatening. The amount of lithium that needs to be taken by any individual can be worked out only by blood tests.

Before starting lithium, blood tests will be taken to make sure that your kidneys are working properly and that the chemicals in your blood are balanced properly. You will be examined and a heart trace will be taken to make sure that your heart is working properly. The action of your thyroid gland will also be tested. If there is evidence of disease of the kidneys or of the heart you may not be able to take lithium.

Once you start lithium, blood tests will be taken at least every week until the dose settles and then every month for three months. After this doctors differ: some take blood tests every two months, others less regularly.

Anything that could make you seriously dehydrated, such as going on holiday to somewhere very hot, diarrhoea, vomiting or starting a new drug – water tablets, for instance – may alter the amount of lithium that you need to take. A blood test will have to be done urgently.

If you are to have an operation you should tell the doctor that you are on lithium because it may have to be stopped.

Side effects

Side effects of lithium therapy may include tiredness, passing more water than usual, a fine tremor of the hands, a dry mouth and a metallic taste in the mouth. Many of these pass with time. These side effects should not be confused with signs that the level in your body is too high. If you have severe shaking of the hands, weakness, diarrhoea, vomiting and confusion, see your doctor or go to an accident and emergency department urgently. You may be suffering from lithium toxicity.

Long-term side effects include weight gain and lithium can also sometimes affect the thyroid gland. As a result of this, some of the blood taken to test the level of lithium will be sent off for thyroid hormone checks a couple of times a year. Low thyroid hormones can be treated by stopping the lithium or by giving thyroid hormone tablets.

Lithium can affect the way that your kidneys function once it has been taken for a while. It can cause you to pass a lot of water and give you a terrible thirst. If this happens, you should see your doctor and you may have to stop taking the lithium.

Lithium in pregnancy

Lithium can harm the growing baby in the early stages of pregnancy so anyone who is on lithium and plans to have a child should see their doctor and arrange to stop taking it.

You can start again after three months because the placenta offers some protection to the baby and the baby is less sensitive to it, but this must be done under the supervision of a doctor. The lithium level must be monitored closely because the amount that is needed will change as the pregnancy goes on. More blood tests will be needed than usual.

After birth the baby is not protected by the placenta; lithium gets into the breast milk and can affect the baby, so women on lithium cannot breast-feed.

Carbamazepine

This is another mood stabiliser. It can be used with lithium or instead of lithium in people who cannot take lithium for one reason or another. Blood tests are taken at least every two weeks for the first two months, and less frequently thereafter. Fever may be an indication of blood problems caused by carbamazepine and so you should consult your doctor if you experience such difficulties.

Sodium valproate

This is a drug that is used for epilepsy and has mood-stabilising functions. In the past, it was used only if neither lithium nor carbamazepine could be given, but now it is the preferred drug of some specialists. Blood tests should be taken regularly.

Other mood stabilisers

Specialists may use drugs that are used in brain conditions such as epilepsy, and which have been shown to have a mood-stabilising action, such as nimodipine, lamotrigine, gabapentin and topiramate.

The hormone thyroxine is also sometimes used in people with rapidly changing high and low moods. These drugs are used only if more common treatments such as lithium, sodium valproate and carbamazepine are ineffective.

Other treatments prescribed for depression
Sleeping pills

Problems with sleep are common in depression. They may result from the depression itself, but this is not always the case. Possible other causes for poor sleep, such as a medical problem or perhaps even a tablet prescribed for a medical problem, should be dealt with.

Stress management and other techniques (see page 52) often help sleep. If the sleep problem is the result of the depression, it will improve with antidepressant treatment. If sleeping problems are troublesome, an antidepressant should be chosen that has a sedative as well as an antidepressant action.

Sometimes it is not possible to prescribe a sedative antidepressant and, if this is the case, a doctor may prescribe an antidepressant and a sleeping pill. Sleeping pills should be used only for a short time – two weeks at most. Some people find them difficult to stop, they become dependent on them and they may suffer withdrawal symptoms. Even if they are prescribed for only a short time, they are best used intermittently.

There are many sleeping pills. Drugs such as temazepam and oxazepam are sometimes prescribed – they are from the same family as Valium (diazepam). There are new sleeping tablets, such as zopiclone, but they work in much the same way as Valium and have the same problem of dependence. Some hayfever tablets, antihistamines, cause drowsiness and are used as sleeping tablets. Sleeping pills do not cure underlying causes of poor sleep.

Anti-anxiety pills

Many people with depression also feel anxious. This is a symptom of the depression and, much like sleep, it gets better when the depression gets better.

If anxiety is severe, doctors may prescribe an anti-anxiety drug with the antidepressant. There are many drugs that are used to treat anxiety, for instance propranolol, Valium (diazepam), buspirone and thioridazine. The use of an antidepressant and an anti-anxiety tablet is best avoided – an antidepressant by itself usually works or an anti-depressant together with psychological treatments. If an anti-anxiety drug is to be prescribed in depression, it should be used only short term.

A one- to two-week course of a Valium-like drug may be prescribed, but this should not be continued for longer as the risk of dependence increases.

For a fuller discussion of anxiety, see the Family Doctor Book *Understanding Anxiety and Panic Attacks*.

Treatment of psychotic depression

People with severe depression may lose touch with reality and develop delusions and hallucinations. In such cases, doctors may prescribe two drugs:

(1) one that has an effect on the depression

(2) one that has an effect on the delusions and hallucinations (an antipsychotic).

Studies have shown that a tricyclic antidepressant and an antipsychotic work better than an antidepressant alone in these cases. Antipsychotic drugs, such as chlorpromazine, trifluoperazine and haloperidol, are very powerful and can have a number of side effects. Newer antipsychotics, such as olanzapine and respiridone, have fewer side effects and are being used by some doctors.

Antipsychotic drugs will usually be prescribed only to control the psychotic symptoms and will then be reduced and stopped, leaving the person on the antidepressant alone.

Which antidepressant should I take?

There are over 30 antidepressants on the market. Different doctors have different opinions as to what is the best antidepressant. This is often not supported by research. Proper research studies show that, in mild/ moderate depression, there is little to choose among the SSRIs, tricyclic and related antidepressants with regard to their effects on symptoms. However, in severe depression treated in hospital, there is some evidence that tricyclic antidepressants are better than SSRIs and, in reverse depression, MAOIs may be more effective.

The choice of antidepressant often depends on other things, for instance, whether a particular drug suits you or whether you have had successful treatment or treatment failure before.

Does the drug suit you?

Different antidepressants have different side effects and different people are vulnerable to different side effects. If you cannot tolerate the side effects of one antidepressant, it may be worth changing your medication. However, you should not keep changing antidepressants; the side effects are usually less troublesome than the depression and the medication works only if you stick at it.

Physical problems such as a heart condition can influence which antidepressant you can be given. You should remind your doctor of any medical condition that you have, so that you will be offered a proper choice of drug.

Newer antidepressants tend not to be used in pregnant or breast-feeding women until there is evidence that they are safe for the baby.

Past treatment

If you have had depression before and it has been successfully treated with an antidepressant, it is best to use the same one. If it worked before, it will work again.

If an antidepressant of one class (for instance, SSRIs) is taken at the correct dose for the correct time and it fails to lift the depression, you should be prescribed a different class of drug (for instance, a tricyclic antidepressant).

This will give the best chance of success. If, however, you do not want to change the type of drug that you are taking or there is some special reason for staying with the same class of drugs (for instance, if you have heart disease, SSRIs are considered best), changing to another drug from the same class can sometimes work.

What happens if you have taken two different antidepressants and they have not worked?

Most people get better if they take the first antidepressant that they are given in the right dose for long enough. The remainder usually get better on the second drug that they are given. A minority of people do not get better even after they have been given two different drugs. If this happens to you, do not despair. There are many alternatives, including:

- using high doses of particular antidepressants

- taking another tablet that boosts the function of the antidepressant that you are taking

- taking a combination of antidepressants.

Some of these changes can be made by your GP, but many will require a referral to a psychiatrist. This is because, if you are given two drugs, they may need special monitoring to which your GP does not have access.

KEY POINTS

■ Antidepressants are an effective treatment

■ Antidepressants are not addictive

■ Side effects can be lessened by starting with low doses or using newer antidepressants

Physical treatment

Electroconvulsive therapy

Electroconvulsive therapy (ECT) is one of the most controversial of psychiatric treatments. It is also one of the most effective. It works, and works quickly, in the vast majority of people (eight of ten) when it is properly prescribed. It has also proven to be safe.

ECT is usually offered to people:

- whose depression has not responded to antidepressants

- who have medical conditions that mean they cannot take antidepressants

- who are so severely depressed that they are endangering their life (say by not eating or drinking at all).

Some doctors offer it to women with very severe postnatal depression because it starts working straight away and means that they can get back to bonding with their child.

Some people who have had ECT before and on whom it works well have it as an outpatient but most people stay in hospital as an inpatient.

The idea of convulsive therapy fills some people with disgust. Critics cannot understand why psychiatrists use such a barbaric treatment. They say that no one knows how ECT works, that it causes permanent problems in the brain and that it is like a form of mediaeval torture which has no place in twentieth century medicine.

The simple truth is that, if it did not work and did not work well, it would not be used. Psychiatrists are doctors whose duty is to their patients. It is true that no one knows how ECT works but there are many treatments that doctors give for all sorts of illnesses that they do not fully understand.

Studies have shown that it does not cause long-term brain problems. Some people have complained of some temporary memory loss, but modifications in the way ECT is given have reduced this. Most people have no memory loss at all and nearly everyone finds that their memory improves as their depression lifts.

ECT does not solve the underlying problems that caused the depression but it does return you to a state whereby you can start looking at these problems. Like taking drugs for depression, ECT will not guarantee that you will stay well. If you have a serious depression you are at risk of a further bout.

What happens in ECT?

An anaesthetist gives you a short-acting anaesthetic to help you sleep and something to relax you. Oxygen is given by facemask while you are asleep. A small electric current is passed through your brain using electrodes

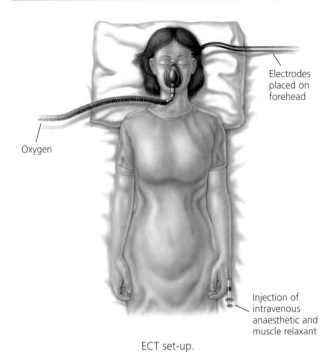

Electrodes placed on forehead

Oxygen

Injection of intravenous anaesthetic and muscle relaxant

ECT set-up.

placed on the scalp. The amount of current given is one-tenth that which is used to start someone's heart if it has stopped. If there was no anaesthetic or muscle relaxant you would have a short fit but because of the anaesthetic all that is seen is some twitching of the toes which lasts a few seconds. This is an indication that the brain has a fit but the body does not. You will wake up 10–15 minutes later. Some people complain that their memory is not so good or they feel slightly confused straight after ECT.

ECT starts to work straight away; most people feel significantly better after a couple of weeks. Most people have six to ten treatments over the course of a few weeks (two to three treatments a week).

Getting ECT

Written consent is needed for ECT just as it is for an operation. If you do not consent it will not usually be given. It can be given against your will only if your life is in danger. Your GP, a specially trained social worker and a psychiatrist must all agree that it is required. Then an independent psychiatrist from the Mental Health Commission will be called in to assess the case. This psychiatrist also has to agree that ECT is required before it can be given and specifies how many sessions can be given. However, if waiting for this psychiatrist to arrive could be dangerous for you the doctors can start treatment.

Transcranial magnetic stimulation

Repetitive transcranial magnetic stimulation is a new technique that some believe could be useful in the treatment of depression. A very strong, pulsed, magnetic field is produced from a hand-held baton, which is held against the head. You can do this yourself – you do not need to be asleep or have an anaesthetic.

The magnetic field affects the nerve cells and some say that it helps to right the chemical imbalance thought to underlie depressive symptoms. Initial studies have shown that it is safe and useful, and some people are using it already and swear by it. However, more studies are needed before it can be recommended.

KEY POINTS

- ECT is given only to people who desperately need it

- It is a safe treatment for depression

- ECT does not lead to brain damage

What happens when you go to your GP?

If you think that you are suffering from depression your GP is the first person whom you should consult. He or she will be able to offer experienced help:

- Your GP will discuss your problems and make sure that they are not the result of a physical illness.

- Your GP will decide how severe your depression is.

- If you have a mild depression, you may not be prescribed medication. You will be given advice, may be offered psychotherapy or counselling, and your GP will see you again to make sure that things get better.

- If you have a moderate depression your GP may offer you antidepressants and may refer you for psychotherapy or counselling.

- If you do not want to take antidepressants your GP will monitor your progress – you should strongly consider taking the tablets if your GP thinks that you need them.

- If you have severe depression your GP may treat you but may refer you to a psychiatrist. This will depend on your symptoms.

- Your GP will want to see you a week or two after starting antidepressants. This is to make sure that you do not have side effects and can take the tablets.

- If you cannot tolerate the drugs they can be changed – so tell your GP if you have problems.

- The pills work gradually; sleep and tiredness improve first – depressed mood often last.

- You will see your GP regularly to get more tablets and to make sure that things are going well.

- After six weeks you should feel much better. All your symptoms may not have gone, but you will be well on the road to recovery. You should continue to improve over the next few weeks.

- Even though you feel much better you should continue to take your tablets for another six months or so. After this you will come off them slowly, not all in one go.

- If you are not better, your GP may increase the dose and see you again in three weeks.

- If you are better, your GP will keep you on the tablets for at least six months before you come off them slowly.

- If you are not better, but you have been taking the tablets as prescribed, most GPs will do one of two things: they will either change the class of tablets (for instance, from a tricyclic antidepressant to an SSRI) or they will refer you to a psychiatrist.

- The psychiatrist will assess you again to make sure that nothing else is causing the depression. If not, you may be offered a different type of medication.

- If you are not better in a month the psychiatrist will consider offering a different drug or a combination of drugs, or admitting you to hospital for investigation and assessment.

- If nothing else works and you are very depressed you may be offered ECT.

- If you are severely depressed from the outset – deluded, suicidal or not eating and drinking – your GP may refer you straight to a psychiatrist. You may be offered admission to hospital so that treatment can be started in a safe environment.

Staying well

Once you have recovered from an episode of depression the challenge is keeping well.

Those who have had one bout of depression are at higher risk of having another bout than those who have never had depression.

There are, however, many ways of decreasing the chance of another bout:

- Gradually try to increase the activities that you enjoy
- Take regular exercise – it helps your mood
- Avoid alcohol and illegal/leisure drugs: both of these make you feel good at the time but later make you feel depressed
- If you get isolated or do not want to feel a burden to your friends, join a self-help group to talk through your problems and feelings
- Use the relaxation techniques in this book whenever you feel stressed (see page 54)
- If you have been to therapy, try to make sure that you use the skills in problem-solving and communication that you were taught
- Two to four top-up sessions of brief psychotherapies, such as cognitive–behavioural therapy, over a 12-month period may decrease the chance of relapse
- Take the medication that you are prescribed for as long as is recommended without missing any
- If you have had one bout of depression you may be recommended to take tablets for six months to a year; if you have had more than one bout of depression you may be advised to stay on medication for at least two years
- If you have recurrent episodes of depression, your doctor may recommend that you start a drug called lithium, which has been proved to reduce the number of episodes of depression that people get
- If you decide that you want to stop or reduce the dose of your medicine, do this only after discussing it with your doctor

Women and depression

Depression and gender

Women are twice as likely as men to be diagnosed with depression. There are a number of possible reasons for this:

- It may just be a reflection of the fact that women are more likely to admit to their feelings than men.

- It may be that male doctors see women as being prone to depression and so diagnose it more often.

- It may just be a reflection of the fact that women go to the doctor more often than men, so doctors have more chance of diagnosing depression.

All of these are important factors but there are also physical differences between men and women that seem to make women more prone to depression. The most important of these is the levels of the sex hormones oestrogen and progesterone. Women have a higher level of these hormones and the levels change during the menstrual cycle, throughout pregnancy and childbirth and at the menopause. The pill, which contains sex hormones, can be a cause of depression.

Menstrual cycle

Levels of progesterone and oestrogen vary through the menstrual cycle. Progesterone is produced on average for only 10 days before a period and then its level drops. It has been implicated as a cause of premenstrual syndrome or PMS (also known as premenstrual tension or PMT) which usually begins a few days before the start of menstruation and usually ends shortly after the onset of menstruation – some symptoms of PMS stop as soon as the period begins.

Not all women have the same combination of PMS symptoms, but tender breasts, feelings of distension and abdominal discomfort, together with irritability, anxiety and depression, are particularly common.

Some doctors believe that PMS symptoms are the result of changes in progesterone levels, others that they are caused by worry. They claim that women who badly want a baby may be hoping that their period will not come and women who do not want a baby hope that their period comes. Both will be worried during the time leading up to their periods. These psychological theories have never been proved!

Although many treatments have been used for PMS, including hormone therapy and water tablets (diuretics), they often do not work very well. Support, sympathy and understanding work best in most cases, and treatment is given only to people with severe symptoms. There are some specialist NHS centres that treat people with severe PMS – occasionally with dramatic improvements.

Depression and motherhood

The levels of oestrogen and progesterone are very high in pregnancy and drop dramatically after the baby is born and this sudden change can sometimes trigger depression. About half of women go through the maternity or baby blues, 15 per cent get mild to moderate postnatal depression and one in 500 experiences severe postnatal depression.

Maternity blues

Half of new mothers suffer from 'maternity blues' in the week after the birth. It's usually around about the third day after the birth that a new mother may start to feel a bit irritable and weepy. Usually she will be back to her old self again by the end of the first week and all she needs in the meantime is support, love and understanding.

Mild and moderate postnatal depression

Long-term depression is common after childbirth. It often goes unnoticed as it is put down to the new mother adjusting to her responsibilities or being kept awake at night by the child. The severest types of depression occur soon after the birth of the baby but the least severe and most common start between two weeks and a year later. Sometimes they may start around the time when the support and attention of friends and family start to wane. The symptoms may be more vague than in other types of depression. Often the woman is very anxious, especially about whether her baby is well and feeding properly, and she may seem to be full of guilt and self-criticism as well as constantly tired and irritable.

Postnatal depression cannot be explained simply by hormone changes. For one thing, the major changes in hormone levels often occur long before the depression begins. It may be that they make a woman prone to depression but social factors are important too.

In general, women are at increased risk of postnatal depression after a particularly difficult pregnancy or birth, when the reality of motherhood or the change in role fall below expectations and/or when having a new baby brings relationship difficulties to the fore.

Treatment is usually needed for postnatal depression. A recent study showed that both anti-depressant drugs and cognitive–behavioural therapy (see page 66) are effective. Most antidepressants can be taken while breast-feeding.

The risk factors for postnatal depression

Certain factors increase the likelihood of the new mother suffering from postnatal depression. The more risk factors that a woman has, the greater her chance of depression.

Before the baby is born

- Fertility problems
- Past psychiatric illness
- Psychiatric illness in the family
- Single parent
- Serious financial problems
- Having a child when very young (under 16 years)
- Having a child when over 35 years of age
- Uncertainty whether you want the baby
- Worries about the baby's health
- Mild-to-moderate anxiety during the last three months of pregnancy
- A difficult labour

After the baby is born

- Pre-term birth (delivery before week 37)
- Physical illness
- Social isolation
- Lack of support from your partner
- Returning to work at a lower level of seniority

When a woman is being treated for postnatal depression, it usually helps if her partner can become involved and understand what is involved. In some cases, fathers may be in need of support too: there is a high risk of depression in new fathers who have depressed partners. Treatment makes a big difference to recovery rate: women who get treatment for postnatal depression are likely to get completely better, whereas those who don't have a 50:50 chance of feeling better by the child's first birthday.

Severe postnatal depression

A more unusual type of postnatal depression affects a minority of women who become severely depressed in the first two weeks after the baby is born. It is more likely:

- after the first pregnancy

- in those who have had a psychiatric illness before

- in those who have psychiatric illness in the family.

It is thought that hormonal change may act as a trigger for depression in those who are prone to it.

In severe depression, a woman loses touch with reality and she may have delusions and hallucinations. There is a real risk to her baby in this situation and mothers who are severely ill have been known to kill their babies. Some depressed women believe that the world is so bad that they should put their child out of its misery, others that there is something wrong with their child and that they are performing a mercy killing.

When the situation is as serious as this, the woman will probably have to be admitted to hospital for treatment, especially if there is a risk that she might harm her baby or herself. The ideal place is a hospital mother and baby unit, where she can be with her baby and have help from the staff to care for him or her.

Treatment is usually with antidepressants and she may also have other types of medication to deal with hallucinations and delusions. It's usually possible to breast-feed while taking medication, but small amounts of drugs do get into the breast milk. When a high dose is required or if the baby is particularly sensitive to the drugs, it may be necessary to switch to bottle-feeding if no other medication is suitable. A mother who is being treated with lithium (see page 83) will have to stop breast-feeding as babies are very sensitive to its effects.

Some doctors offer electroconvulsive therapy for severe depression after childbirth. It works quickly and enables the new mother to get on with bonding with her child. The vast majority of women are treated with tablets.

If you have had postnatal depression you are likely to make a good recovery but you will be at risk of developing it after any future pregnancies. You should tell your doctor or obstetrician that you have had postnatal depression before you have your next baby so that you can be monitored and receive early and prompt treatment if you need it.

The menopause

Women are more likely to seek help for depression around their middle years. Many doctors believe that this is due to the menopause (a woman's last menstrual period). The theory is that hormone level changes spark depression as they can do after childbirth or with premenstrual syndrome. However, there is no reliable evidence that depression is actually more common at the time of the menopause.

There are, of course, a number of other changes that happen in many women's lives in middle age which may be playing a role in triggering depression. For example, children leave home, the relationship with their partner may change and their own parents may become ill.

In the UK, women who have a depressive illness and happen to be around the time of the menopause will be treated with antidepressants if appropriate, just like anyone else with a similar condition. However, in the USA, psychiatrists are more convinced that hormones are the cause and some prescribe treatment with oestrogens. It is unclear whether they work, but some women in this country who are prescribed hormone replacement therapy (which includes oestrogen) for menopausal symptoms say that they also feel less depressed while taking it.

Hysterectomy and sterilisation

Research from some years ago claimed that women were more likely to become depressed after either being sterilised or having a hysterectomy, but recent research has cast doubt on this. The ovaries produce a number of hormones with functions that are not clear and some doctors in the USA say that, in some women, their removal will cause depression. Other doctors say that hysterectomy sets off depression only in a woman who is already predisposed to psychiatric illness, while some experts point out that there are some women who actually recover from psychiatric symptoms after a hysterectomy.

The same applies to sterilisation operations. In other words, it may be only women who were at risk of depression who will develop the illness after being sterilised.

Women at home

Women may have a higher rate of depression because of their social situation rather than because of anything to do with their hormones. In a landmark study researchers in south London surveyed women who were at home during the day.

They found that the most likely people to be depressed were young mothers with three or more children under the age of ten, with an unsupportive partner, no one else to confide in, poorly housed and having no employment outside the home.

KEY POINTS

- There are many reasons why women are diagnosed with depression more often than men

- Changes in oestrogen and progesterone may trigger depression

- Depression after childbirth is often missed but can be treated effectively

Depression in young people

Symptoms of depression in young people
There are many similarities between depression in children and depression in adults but there are also important differences.

Many of the symptoms of depression are the same in young people as they are in adults. As with adults, there is a change in mood that persists over time. There are physical symptoms such as poor sleep or too much sleep and low energy levels, and there are psychological symptoms such as poor concentration, and a negative view of the world and their place in it.

However, many young people will deny feeling sad even though their behaviour has changed, and they will be more grumpy or irritable. There is no consistent way in which depression in children shows itself. Some come to the attention of GPs because they complain of headaches, stomach pains or bone pain but no cause can be found. Others present for the first time with self-harm, disinterest in general appearance, withdrawal and loss of interest, but in others a change in behaviour such as a decline in schoolwork or increased argumentativeness is the first sign.

Symptoms of depression vary according to age. Children are more likely to complain of physical problems such as headaches and abdominal pains and tend not to look depressed. Adolescents are more likely to complain of low mood and to have a higher rate of suicidal thoughts.

Moody or depressed?

National surveys have shown that many young people have some depressive symptoms but they are not serious enough to be considered an illness or need treatment.

Trying to disentangle depression from normal mood problems in teenagers can be difficult. One indication is that depressed teenagers often no longer derive pleasure from life and have poor self-esteem. They may have little to say when asked about their good points, they think that they are no good and that the situation in which they find themselves is their fault, but they do not have the ability to change things. When this is coupled with the adult symptoms of depression, such as poor concentration, loss of confidence and in severe cases delusions and suicidal thoughts, the diagnosis is not too difficult.

Depressive illness is diagnosed when the symptoms lead to significant personal suffering and social impairment.

It often takes time to make the diagnosis. As with adults, many young people are not forthcoming when seeing a doctor or therapist. As with adults depression can also be considered as mild, moderate or severe, depending on the number and intensity of symptoms that are present.

One rule of thumb is that depression needs treating only if it stops someone from doing things that they want to or changes their ability to do things, for instance interferes with their schoolwork. Otherwise minor symptoms can just be monitored.

Risk factors and figures

Depression is less common in young people than it is in adults. Each year one per cent of pre-pubertal children and three per cent of post-pubertal adolescents suffer from depression.

Some of the underlying causes of depression in children are similar to the causes for depression in adult life, for instance genes, personality or family environment. Others, such as bullying, being put into care, personality and social development in adolescence and changes in hormones and brain development, are specific to young people.

More than 95 per cent of major depressive episodes in young people arise in children and young people with long-standing difficulties, such as family or marital disharmony, divorce and separation, domestic violence, physical and sexual abuse, school difficulties and exam failure.

A very small number of depressive episodes in children and young people will arise in the absence of prior difficulties, and result from an acute life event such as a mugging.

Depression is triggered by an event that has a high negative impact, for instance parental separation or getting into relationship difficulties with a close friend.

Social stress seems to be an important underlying factor because the rates of depression are higher in poorer households, households with single parents, in families where parents did less well at school and in children who are in local authority care or young offender institutions.

Depression in children and young people tends to occur in conjunction with other mental health problems such as abuse of drugs or alcohol or hyperactivity.

Treatment of depression in childhood

Most young people who are depressed do not get treatment. This is because they are reluctant to seek help as a result of the stigma of mental health problems, but they also do not get help because depression is missed by parents, health professionals and teachers. Depression is missed in three-quarters of young people who suffer from it.

Some high-risk groups for childhood depression

- Those who refuse to go to school
- Abused children
- Young people who have experienced a significant traumatic event
- Young people who repeatedly harm themselves
- Young people in chronic family disputes
- Young people with persistent drug and alcohol problems.

Treatment strategies should be aimed at the whole child. Many young people with depression suffer from other mental health problems and there are often social and family issues, so everything has to be dealt with. Attention should be paid to the possible need for treatment of the parents' own psychiatric problems, for instance depression.

A treatment programme should aim to:

- cure the depression

- improve other mental health problems

- improve social and emotional development and school performance

- decrease family distress

- reduce the risk of relapse.

Treatment for depression in young people can occur at one of three levels.

Level 1

Services include GPs, paediatricians, health visitors, school nurses and social workers

Level 2

Services include child and adolescent mental health services such as clinical child psychologists, paediatricians with specialist training in mental health, educational psychologists, child and adolescent psychiatrists, child and adolescent psychotherapists, counsellors and family therapists.

Level 3

Services include child and adolescent psychiatry day units, highly specialised outpatient teams and inpatient units (inpatients are hospitalised, outpatients receive treatment at a hospital but then return home).

Most young people with depression are treated in level 1 and 2 services. Very few are ever admitted to a specialist inpatient unit.

Mild depression

Mild depression in young people is usually treated by a family doctor and other level 1 services. Most GPs will assess the young person and the family. A good GP will give the patient the opportunity to be seen alone as well as with a parent.

If after assessment there are considered to be complicating factors, for example other significant risk factors such as suicidal thoughts, mental health problems such as substance misuse or mental health problems in other family members, the GP may decide to refer direct to level 2 services.

In cases where there is no indication of suicidal thoughts or any other significant problem GPs usually start with watchful waiting – seeing the person again in two weeks and then after another two weeks to see whether the depression rights itself.

If after a month of watchful waiting, things have not improved then one of three interventions will usually be offered for up to three months:

(1) individual supportive psychotherapy

(2) group cognitive–behavioural therapy

(3) guided self-help (see box on page 118).

Guided self-help for mild depression

Guided self-help should include:

- Books and educational leaflets about depression
- Advice on the benefits of regular exercise and a supervised exercise programme (three sessions per week of 45 minutes to 1 hour for up to three months)
- Advice on achieving good quality sleep and anxiety management
- Advice on nutrition and the benefits of a balanced diet

Antidepressant medication should not be used for the initial treatment of children and young people with mild depression.

If after three months of treatment the depression has not responded a specialist opinion is needed.

Moderate-to-severe depression

Most GPs refer young people with depression to a child and adolescent psychiatric service only if they have complex problems, if they have not responded to three months of treatment or if from the outset they have moderate-to-severe depression, recurrence of depression, suicidal ideas or plans or unexplained self-neglect of at least one month's duration. However, if you ask for a referral most GPs will oblige.

Children and young people with moderate-to-severe depression should be offered, as a first-line treatment, a specific psychological therapy such as individual cognitive–behavioural therapy, interpersonal therapy or family therapy for at least three months. If this does not work additional therapy on a one-to-one basis for the young person or parents may be considered.

Given the complex and serious nature of depression, a number of professionals may be involved, each trying to improve a specific aspect of the problem. For instance, in addition to a psychiatrist, educational psychologists may be helping with school, family therapists with family difficulties, and social workers with financial, housing or legal problems.

Medication

If psychological therapies are not effective, doctors may consider adding medication to the treatment. Antidepressant medication should be offered only in combination with psychological therapies. If psychological therapies are refused antidepressants can be prescribed alone but there needs to be close monitoring – preferably weekly for at least the first four weeks. This is because side effects need to be assessed and because in some young people antidepressants make them feel more suicidal.

In those aged over 12 there is some evidence that one drug – fluoxetine, an SSRI (selective serotonin release inhibitor) – is effective. In the 5- to 11-year-old group the evidence that any drug is effective is sparse. If fluoxetine is not effective another antidepressant may be tried.

Admission to a hospital

Admission to a hospital unit for level 3 services may be considered if the child/young person is at high risk of suicide, serious self-harm and self-neglect, the required intensity of treatment (or supervision) is not available in the community or intensive assessment is needed.

Antidepressant treatment in children

- Antidepressants should be offered only in combination with psychological therapy
- Antidepressants should be prescribed in low doses
- Antidepressants may be given if psychological therapies are refused but there should be close monitoring of mood and side effects
- Antidepressants should be prescribed only after assessment and diagnosis by a child and adolescent psychiatrist
- Fluoxetine should usually be prescribed in the UK because the National Institute for Health and Clinical Excellence decided that it is the only antidepressant for which trials show that benefits outweigh risks
- If fluoxetine does not work, other antidepressants may be used after careful consideration and discussion, but British doctors are advised not to prescribe paroxetine, venlafaxine and tricyclic antidepressants
- All antidepressants must be monitored for side effects and for the possible development of suicidal thoughts
- Antidepressants should be continued for six months after symptoms have gone
- Medication should be stopped slowly over a 6- to 12-week period
- If a young person is taking St John's wort, he or she should be advised to stop taking it

Once depression has resolved

A young person who has suffered from depression is at increased risk of another bout. As a result of this services will usually keep an eye on the person for at least a year after the depression has resolved. In addition, they will fast-track them if symptoms return.

What is the outlook?

Depression in children is a serious illness. With no treatment only ten per cent will recover within three months. Leave it for a year and half will have recovered. Treatment decreases the duration of the illness.

The most serious complication of depression is suicide with three per cent of depressed children killing themselves within the next ten years; other problems are poor school performance and difficulties in personality development. One in three young people with depression has a recurrence within five years and many develop episodes into adult life.

KEY POINTS

- Many of the symptoms of depression are the same in young people as they are in adults

- Depression in young people is often triggered by an event that has a high negative impact – for example, parental separation

- Treatment for depression in young people can occur at one of three levels

- Antidepressant medication should not be used for the initial treatment of young people with mild depression

Grief and bereavement

The link between bereavement and depression

There is a complex link between bereavement and depression. Bereavement can trigger a depressive illness, though it usually does not. However, a recently bereaved person can experience many symptoms that are similar to depression. In one study, about 30 per cent of recently bereaved widows over the age of 62 were found to meet criteria for depressive illness.

In bereavement suicidal thoughts, mental and physical slowness and worry about past actions are much less likely to occur. If you suffer from these you may be depressed rather than just grieving and treatment may be needed. If you have thoughts of self-harm or completely stop eating you should see a doctor urgently.

Normal grief

Grief is a normal experience; it is painful but does not need medical treatment. There are three stages.

1. Numbness
This lasts from a few hours to one week. You may feel emotionally numb and feel as if the person hasn't died or that you can't accept the reality of their death.

2. Mourning
From one week to six months (easier after about three months). You may feel sad, depressed, have little appetite, find yourself crying a lot, or be agitated, anxious and have little concentration. Some people feel guilty. They feel that they had not done enough for the deceased. Others blame professionals or friends and family. You may find that you have physical symptoms such as pains during this phase.

Most people have the feeling at some time during this stage that the deceased is present in some way and one in ten report either seeing, hearing or smelling the dead person when they are not there. Many of the experiences mimic depression but they are normal – you are not depressed or going mad.

3. Acceptance
Six months onwards. Symptoms subside. You start to accept the death and try to get back to normal. This takes a variable time.

Coping with grief
Grief is natural and so are your feelings. Grief is a process that has to be worked through. If it is not, then feelings could fester and they could catch up on you in the end turning into depression. Grief should not be bottled up and needs to be let out.

Even if you seem to be having a severe reaction to the death at first, you are likely to come through the

process with just the support of your friends and family or a counsellor.

It is usually best to turn to your family and friends initially. They will all need to grieve themselves and the help and support that they offer you will help them to come to terms with what has happened. You are not a burden, it is a two-way thing. They need you as well.

Counsellors can offer support in grief and can help people work through the process in a controlled way. They are particularly useful if you find that you are not passing through the stages of grief or you are having a particularly difficult time. Bereavement counsellors aim to help you acknowledge the death by helping you talk about the circumstances surrounding it; they

Causes of intense grief

Although the death of a loved one is always hard to bear, certain situations make the grief even more intense:

- If the death is sudden or unexpected
- If the death results in blame for the survivor
- When a parent's child dies
- When a young child's parent dies
- When an adult was dependent on the person who died
- When the survivor has difficulties expressing his or her feelings
- When the survivor is currently still adapting to a previous loss
- When the survivor is socially isolated
- When the survivor has dependent children

encourage emotional expression of the pain of grief; they try to identify coping strategies and people who might offer support; they help the process of building a new life and help you let go of the dead person. You can contact such counsellors through your GP, or ring CRUSE or other self-help groups listed under 'Useful information', page 136.

Supporting someone who is grieving

Giving space for a grieving person to talk about their feelings is all important. Most people think that they need to say how wonderful the deceased was but that is often not the support that someone needs:

- They need space to talk about how they feel.
- They need to be allowed to say;
  - how bad they feel.
  - how distressed they are.
  - how they might feel guilty.
  - how they feel angry that they have been left behind.
  - how they said something bad before the person died.
  - how the death brings their own mortality closer.

All these thoughts and feelings are normal and need expression.

Medication

Medication can be counterproductive early on in the grieving process. Though drugs may make you feel better they may interfere with the process of grieving and prolong it. It is painful to work through the feelings of loss but it is the only way to get back to normal.

If you really cannot sleep at all for the first few days your GP may prescribe tranquillisers. This will be for only a few days to help you sleep and then they will be stopped. In extreme circumstances these may be useful for a few critical days but should not be used long term. Though they may help you to feel better they will not help you work through your grief and you will have to do this when you stop taking the tablets. It is only if grief turns into depression that drug treatment has any place long term.

Self-help

There are a number of self-help organisations that

can offer advice and support, including CRUSE Bereavement Care, the Terrence Higgins Trust and Compassionate Friends. For a full listing see 'Useful information' on page 136.

Abnormal grief

Not everybody passes through the stages of grief smoothly. Some people find that they do not pass through the normal stages and suffer persistent problems. Others find it difficult to grieve and do not acknowledge the death at all. Some people find that they are consumed with intense anger or feelings of betrayal which last for months. If grief is intense and unbearable it needs to be treated. Contact your GP or counsellors such as those at CRUSE.

KEY POINTS

- Grief is a normal reaction

- Medication is not usually needed and may be counterproductive

- Self-help organisations provide excellent bereavement counselling

Helping friends and family

The value of talking and listening

If you are able to recognise when someone is depressed and offer support, your help will be priceless. You may not think that you have done very much but you will have helped someone in need and may even have helped prevent a suicide.

Many people who are depressed find it difficult to take up offers of help so don't be put off. Try to be patient and tell them that you are ready to talk when they want to.

When you do talk, be sympathetic, be supportive and try to convince them to see their GP. There is no point telling a person who is depressed to snap out of it or to pull themselves together. Nobody likes being depressed and they would snap out of it if they could.

Talking allows people to work through their problems, but listening is not easy. It can be uncomfortable, especially when someone you know is distressed and they are saying things that are either

not true or so painful that you do not know how to cope with the emotions that they produce in you. Do not take on too much.

Try not to give quick ungrounded reassurance or quick advice and don't think that you have to say something because you feel uncomfortable. Do not jump in and interrupt – give them time and space to say what they feel. Accept that they feel the way they do and see the world the way that they do. If you think that they are wrong explain why you think so and give them proof but do not get into an argument. You will be doing a good job if you listen, acknowledge how the person feels, be sympathetic and hold back on giving too much advice.

Remember, you can assure them that medical treatment is effective and that they will get better.

Once you have talked things through, try to keep in touch, be accessible and offer practical help and support until they are better. Helping people to get help by offering to accompany them to a GP appointment can be useful but be careful not to take over. Many people with depression feel ineffective and taking over their decisions may make them feel worse.

Preventing suicide

Of the 5,000 suicides in England and Wales each year about 3,000 are the result of depression. Most people suffering from depression get better. The box on page 134 lists groups of people who are at high risk but it should be borne in mind that anyone who is seriously depressed may be thinking about suicide and you should be vigilant.

Attempts at suicide are not just a way of getting attention and they should always be taken seriously. Of course there are people who try to harm themselves as a cry for help – but if that cry goes unheard, goes wrong or is in the context of a depression then it could herald suicide.

Knowing about depression, ensuring that someone who is depressed gets treatment and keeping in touch are important.

Supporting someone who is suicidal without professional help is very difficult. If you are at all worried you should try to convince the sufferer to see someone as soon as possible. They can go to their GP, go into any accident and emergency department, or it may be possible to arrange for a doctor or nurse to come to see them at home. Your local psychiatric department may have an emergency clinic that you can just walk into.

Helping a friend who is suicidal

If you suspect that a person is suicidal talk with them and let them speak about their feelings. Ask them if they have ever thought that it was not worth going on. Some may say yes and that they have thought of taking their own life; others may say that they have not thought of it but they have gone to bed at night hoping that they would not wake up. Both groups of people are potential suicide risks.

Of course some people intent on suicide will deny that they have thought of it; you may have to make a judgement as to whether they are telling the truth. Many people find speaking about their suicidal impulses is a tremendous release and it may actually stop them going through with it.

If you do not live with them make sure that they have your telephone number, and the numbers of their GP, the Samaritans and other caring agencies. Arrange a definite time when you will see them again. This could be in an hour or two or the next day depending on how they are.

If you can get their agreement to remove paracetamol, large quantities of antidepressant or non-essential drugs from their medicine cupboard, this would be a good move.

If you are worried that your friend is in imminent danger do not leave them while you are getting in contact with helping agencies if at all possible.

It is always best to discuss what you are doing with the sufferer. They will probably agree that they should see someone, but if they do not and you really think that they are a danger to themselves, you should act in their interests. If you think you should, you should contact the GP, the Samaritans or their family. You can contact the local psychiatric outpatients and see if there is a walk-in clinic. You can take them to an accident and emergency department.

If you feel suicidal – seek help. Speak to someone urgently. Talk it over with your partner, a friend, your GP, the Samaritans – anybody.

Factors that increase suicide risk

The likelihood of a person committing suicide is increased if any of the following conditions or categories applies:

- Severe depression
- Serious physical illness accompanying depression
- Person has spoken about suicide
- Past suicide attempt
- Suicide in the family
- Continuing severe life stresses such as divorce or bereavement
- People who are lonely and socially isolated
- Men, who are more likely to succeed in their suicide attempt
- Unemployed individuals
- People taking illicit drugs
- Those with alcohol problems

KEY POINTS

- Listening may be the most important thing that you can do for family and friends who are depressed

- Anyone who thinks about suicide should contact their GP, accident and emergency department at their local hospital or the Samaritans, and get help

- Depression can be treated – you will feel better

Useful information

We have included the following organisations because, on preliminary investigation, they may be of use to the reader. However, we do not have first-hand experience of each organisation and so cannot guarantee the organisation's integrity. The reader must therefore exercise his or her own discretion and judgement when making further enquiries.

Association for Postnatal Illness
145 Dawes Road
London SW6 7EB
Tel: 020 7386 0868 (Mon, Wed Fri 10am–2pm; Tues, Thurs 10am–5pm)
Fax: 020 7386 8885
Email: info@apni.org
Website: www.apni.org

Offers information and advice to sufferers and their families, and can put people in touch with others who have had similar problems.

Benefits Enquiry Line
Tel: 0800 882200
Minicom: 0800 243355
Website: www.dwp.gov.uk
N. Ireland: 0800 220674

Government agency giving information and advice on sickness and disability benefits for people with disabilities and their carers.

British Association for Counselling and Psychotherapy
BACP House, 35–37 Albert Street
Rugby CV21 2SG
Tel: 0870 443 5252
Fax: 0870 443 5161
Minicom: 0870 443 5162
Email: bacp@bacp.co.uk
Website: www.bacp.co.uk

Provides a directory listing counsellors and the types of problems for which they offer counselling. Enquirers can be referred to an experienced local counsellor.

British Complementary Medicine Association
PO Box 5122
Bournemouth BH8 0WG
Tel/Fax: 0845 345 5977
Email: info@bcma.co.uk
Website: www.bcma.co.uk

Multi-therapy umbrella body representing organisations, clinics, colleges and independent schools, and acting as the voice of complementary medicine. Offers lists of qualified and insured practitioners of complementary medicine.

Compassionate Friends
53 North Street
Bristol BS3 1EN
Tel: 0845 120 3785
Fax: 0845 120 3786
Helpline: 0845 123 2304 (10am–4pm, 6.30–10.30pm, 365 days a year)
Email: info@tcf.org.uk
Website: www.tcf.org.uk

Offers support, information and befriending by bereaved parents for bereaved parents, siblings and close family members.

Cruse (Bereavement Care)
Cruse House, 126 Sheen Road
Richmond, Surrey TW9 1UR
Helpline: 0870 167 1677
Young persons' helpline: 0808 808 1677
Tel: 020 8939 9530
Fax: 020 8940 7638
Bereavement line: 0845 758 5565
Email: helpline@crusebereavementcare.org.uk
Website: www.crusebereavementcare.org.uk

Offers practical and emotional advice after a bereavement. Can provide one-to-one counselling locally and training in bereavement care for professionals.

Depression Alliance
212 Spitfire Studios, 63–71 Collins Street
London N1 9BE
Info line: 0845 123 2320
Email: information@depressionalliance.org
Website: www.depressionalliance.org

Offers support and understanding to anyone affected
by depression and for relatives who want to help.
Has a network of self-help groups, correspondence
schemes and a range of literature; send an SAE for
information.

Depression Alliance, Scotland
3 Grosvenor Gardens
Edinburgh EH12 5JU
Tel: 0131 467 3050 (Mon, Tues, Thurs, Fri 10am–2pm)
Fax: 0131 467 7701
Email: info@dascot.org
Website: www.dascot.org

Provides information and support and has local self-
help groups in Scotland.

Depression Alliance, Cymru (Wales)
11 Plas Melin, Westbourne Road
Whitchurch, Cardiff CF14 2BT
Tel: 029 2069 2891
Email: admin@dacymru.org
Website: www.dacymru.ik.com

Provides information and support and has local self-
help groups in Wales.

Fellowship of Depressives Anonymous

Box FDA, Self Help Nottingham, Ormiston House,
32–36 Pelham Street
Nottingham NG1 2EG
Tel: 0870 774 4320
Fax: 0870 774 4319
Email: fdainfo@hotmail.com
Website: www.depressionanon.co.uk

Self-help groups in England for people who suffer from depression and their carers, offering support complementary to professional care. Membership offers newsletters, pen-friend and phone-friend schemes.

First Steps to Freedom

1 Taylor Close
Kenilworth, Warwicks CV8 2LW
Tel/fax: 01926 864 473
Helpline: 0845 120 2916 (10am–10pm, 365 days a year)
Email: first.steps@btconnect.com
Website: www.first-steps.org

Charity offering information and telephone self-help for people with anxiety disorders with practical advice on how to overcome panic attacks, obsessive–compulsive disorders and withdrawal from tranquillisers.

Gay Bereavement Project

c/o Terrence Higgins Trust Counselling
111–117 Lancaster Road
London W11 1QT

Tel: 020 7403 5969 (Tuesday 7–10pm)
Website: www.tht.org.uk

Offers support and counselling for bereavement and
AIDS.

MDF The Bipolar Organisation (Manic Depression Fellowship)

Castle Works, 21 St George's Road
London SE1 6ES
Tel: 020 7793 2600
Fax: 020 7793 2639
Helpline: 0845 634 0540
Email: mdf@mdf.org.uk
Website: www.mdf.org.uk
Website for young people: www.steady.org.uk

Offers support, via self-help groups, to enable people
affected by bipolar disorder/manic depression to take
control of their lives. Has 24-hour legal advice line,
travel insurance and life assurance schemes, self-
management training programme and employment
advice.

Mental Health Foundation

9th Floor, Sea Containers House, 20 Upper Ground
London SE1 9QB
Tel: 020 7803 1100
Fax: 020 7803 1111
Email: mhf@mhf.org.uk
Website: www.mentalhealth.org.uk

Charity working with mental health and learning
disabilities. Includes news, events, resources, research

news and a forum that you can join to discuss mental health.

MIND (National Association for Mental Health)
Granta House, 15–19 Broadway
London E15 4BQ
Mind infoline: 0845 7660 163
Tel: 020 8519 2122
Fax: 020 8522 1725
Email: contact@mind.org.uk
Website: www.mind.org.uk

Works for a better life for anyone experiencing mental distress. Offers support via local branches, drop-in centres, counselling, advocacy, employment and training schemes. Special legal service to the public, lawyers and mental health workers. Publications available on 0844 448 4448.

National Childbirth Trust
Alexandra House, Oldham Terrace
London W3 6NH
Tel: 0870 770 3236
Helpline: 0870 444 8707
Fax: 0870 770 3237
Email: enquiries@national-childbirth-trust.co.uk
Website: www.nctpregnancyandbabycare.com

Self-help organisation offering education, support and advice before and after birth through local groups. Breast-feeding line 0870 444 8708 available 7 days a week 8am–10pm with breast-feeding counsellors.

National Phobics Society (NPS)

Zion Community Resource Centre, 339 Stretford Road
Hulme, Manchester M15 4ZY
Helpline: 0870 122 2325
Fax: 0161 227 9862
Email: nationalphobic@btconnect.com
Website: www.phobics-society.org.uk

Provides information and advice to all those affected
by anxiety disorders and can refer to support groups
and trained hypnotherapists, cognitive therapists and
other complementary therapists.

National Institute for Health and Clinical Excellence (NICE)

MidCity Place, 71 High Holborn
London WC1V 6NA
Tel: 020 7067 5800
Fax: 020 7067 5801
Email: nice@nice.nhs.uk
Website: www.nice.org.uk

Provides national guidance on the promotion of good
health and the prevention and treatment of ill-health.
Patient information leaflets are available for each piece
of guidance issued.

Prodigy Website

Sowerby Centre for Health Informatics
at Newcastle (SCHIN)
Bede House, All Saints Business Centre
Newcastle upon Tyne NE1 2ES
Tel: 0191 243 6100
Fax: 0191 243 6101

Email: prodigy-enquiries@schin.co.uk
Website: www.prodigy.nhs.uk/portal/
PatientInformation/Index.spx

A website mainly for GPs giving information for patients
listed by disease plus named self-help organisations.

Relate

National Office, Herbert Gray College
Little Church Street, Rugby CV21 3AP
Helpline: 0845 130 4010
Tel: 01788 573241
Fax: 01788 535007
Email: enquiries@relate.org.uk
Website: www.relate.org.uk

Offers relationship counselling via local branches.
Relate publications on health, sexual, self-esteem,
depression, bereavement and re-marriage issues
available from bookshops, libraries or via website.

Royal College of Psychiatrists

17 Belgrave Square
London SW1X 8PG
Tel: 020 7235 2351
Fax: 020 7245 1231
Email: rcpsych@rcpsych.ac.uk
Website: www.rcpsych.ac.uk

Professional body holding lists of qualified psychiatrists.
Patients must be referred by GPs. Publishes fact sheets,
books and patient leaflets on mental health and
growing up, about all aspects of child and mental
health problems, advice for parents.

SAD (Seasonal Affective Disorder) Association
PO Box 989
Steyning, W. Sussex BN44 3HG
Tel: 01903 814942
Fax: 01903 879939
Website: www.sada.org.uk

Offers support and information on seasonal affective
disorder and details of light therapy and equipment.
Enquiries by letter welcomed; an SAE requested.

Samaritans HQ
The Upper Mill, Kingston Road
Ewell KT17 2AF
Helpline: 0845 790 9090 (24 hours, 365 days a year)
Tel: 020 8394 8300
Fax: 020 8394 8301
Email: jo@samaritans.org
Website: www.samaritans.org

Offer confidential telephone support to people who
feel suicidal or despairing and need someone to talk
to. Local branches listed in telephone directory. Most
also see visitors at certain times of day.

SANE
First Floor, Cityside House, 40 Adler Street
London E1 1EE
Helpline: 0845 767 8000 (12 noon–11pm; Sat, Sun 12
noon–6pm)
Tel: 020 7375 1002
Fax: 020 7375 2162
Email: info@sane.org.uk
Website: www.sane.org.uk

Offers emotional and crisis support to people with mental health problems, their families and friends; also information for professionals and organisations working in the field. Has database of local and national services.

Terrence Higgins Trust
52–54 Gray's Inn Road
London WC1X 8JU
Tel: 020 7831 0330
Fax: 020 7242 0121
Helpline: 0845 12 21 200 (Mon–Fri 10am–10pm; Sat, Sun 12 noon–6pm; outside hours 07957 812691)
Email: info@tht.org.uk
Website: www.tht.org.uk

Leading HIV charity offering information, advice and support to anyone who is at risk, living with or affected by HIV.

Triumph Over Phobia (TOP UK)
PO Box 3760
Bristol BS2 3WY
Tel: 0845 600 9601
Fax: 0117 956 3907
Email: info@triumphoverphobia.org.uk
Website: www.triumphoverphobia.com

Structured self-help groups for phobia and obsessive–compulsive disorder sufferers. An SAE requested for further information.

Useful information for young people

Childline
Helpline: 0800 1111
Website: www.childline.org.uk

Free and confidential telephone service for children.

YoungMinds
48–50 St John Street
London EC1M 4DG
Parents' information: 0800 018 2138
Website: www.youngminds.org.uk

Information and advice on child mental health issues.

Mental Health and Growing Up
Series of 36 factsheets on a range of common mental
health problems. Download them from
www.rcpsych.ac.uk.

Websites
There are lots of websites and information. Here are
some that should offer most of the information and
links that you need. You can also visit the websites of
the organisations listed above. Many of these will have
useful information and resources that you can
download.

NHS Direct
www.nhsdirect.nhs.uk
Has general advice on depression as well as a useful
health encyclopaedia. Links to depression sites.

www.social-anxiety.org.uk

Voluntary-led website providing information, chat room and local self-help groups.

www.changingminds.co.uk

Changing Minds: Mental Health: What it is, What to do, Where to go?
A multi-media CD-ROM on mental health that looks at depression.

Calm

www.thecalmzone.net
Calm stands for campaign against living miserably. Aimed at young men aged 15–35. Works with people from the music, sports and club scenes to attempt to help people open up and talk about their problems. Currently based in Merseyside but likely to go national in March 2006.

www.thesite.org/info/healthandwellbeing/ mentalhealth/depression

Part of one of the biggest sites for 16–18 year olds. The site is run by the charity Youthnet. It is well maintained with lots of information and advice and the facility to email questions. It is supported by major mental health charities.

Books

Depression: The way out of your prison, by Dorothy Rowe. Routledge, 2003.

Breaking the Bonds: Understanding depression, finding freedom, by Dorothy Rowe. HarperCollins, 1996.

Malignant Sadness: The anatomy of depression, by Lewis Wolpert. Faber & Faber, 2001.

The internet as a source of further information

After reading this book, you may feel that you would like further information on the subject. The internet is of course an excellent place to look and there are many websites with useful information about medical disorders, related charities and support groups.

For those who do not have a computer at home some bars and cafes offer facilities for accessing the internet. These are listed in the *Yellow Pages* under 'Internet Bars and Cafes' and 'Internet Providers'. Your local library offers a similar facility and has staff to help you find the information that you need.

It should always be remembered, however, that the internet is unregulated and anyone is free to set up a website and add information to it. Many websites offer impartial advice and information that has been compiled and checked by qualified medical professionals. Some, on the other hand, are run by commercial organisations with the purpose of promoting their own products. Others still are run by pressure groups, some of which will provide carefully assessed and accurate information whereas others may be suggesting medications or treatments that are not supported by the medical and scientific community.

Unless you know the address of the website you want to visit – for example, www.familydoctor.co.uk – you may find the following guidelines useful when searching the internet for information.

Search engines and other searchable sites

Google (www.google.co.uk) is the most popular search engine used in the UK, followed by Yahoo! (http://uk.yahoo.com) and MSN (www.msn.co.uk). Also popular are the search engines provided by Internet Service Providers such as Tiscali and other sites such as the BBC site (www.bbc.co.uk).

In addition to the search engines that index the whole web, there are also medical sites with search facilities, which act almost like mini-search engines, but cover only medical topics or even a particular area of medicine. Again, it is wise to look at who is responsible for compiling the information offered to ensure that it is impartial and medically accurate. The NHS Direct site (www.nhsdirect.nhs.uk) is an example of a searchable medical site.

Links to many British medical charities can be found at the Association of Medical Research Charities' website (www.amrc.org.uk) and at Charity Choice (www.charitychoice.co.uk).

Search phrases

Be specific when entering a search phrase. Searching for information on 'cancer' will return results for many different types of cancer as well as on cancer in general. You may even find sites offering astrological information. More useful results will be returned by using search phrases such as 'lung cancer' and 'treatments for lung cancer'. Both Google and Yahoo! offer an advanced search option that includes the ability to search for the exact phrase; enclosing the search phrase in quotes, that is, 'treatments for lung cancer', will have the same effect. Limiting a search to an exact phrase reduces the number of results returned but it is best to refine a search to an exact match only if you are not getting useful results with a normal search. Adding 'UK' to your search term will bring up mainly British sites, so a good phrase might be 'lung cancer' UK (don't include UK within the quotes).

Always remember the internet is international and unregulated. It holds a wealth of valuable information but individual sites may be biased, out of date or just plain wrong. Family Doctor Publications accepts no responsibility for the content of links published in this series.

Index

Your pages

We have included the following pages because they may help you manage your illness or condition and its treatment.

Before an appointment with a health professional, it can be useful to write down a short list of questions of things that you do not understand, so that you can make sure that you do not forget anything.

Some of the sections may not be relevant to your circumstances.

We are always pleased to receive constructive criticism or suggestions about how to improve the books. You can contact us at:

Email: familydoctor@btinternet.com
Letter: Family Doctor Publications
        PO Box 4664
        Poole
        BH15 1NN

Thank you

Health-care contact details

Name:

Job title:

Place of work:

Tel:

Name:

Job title:

Place of work:

Tel:

Name:

Job title:

Place of work:

Tel:

Name:

Job title:

Place of work:

Tel:

Significant past health events – illnesses/operations/investigations/treatments

Event	Month	Year	Age (at time)

Appointments for health care

Name:

Place:

Date:

Time:

Tel:

Name:

Place:

Date:

Time:

Tel:

Name:

Place:

Date:

Time:

Tel:

Name:

Place:

Date:

Time:

Tel:

Appointments for health care

Name:

Place:

Date:

Time:

Tel:

Name:

Place:

Date:

Time:

Tel:

Name:

Place:

Date:

Time:

Tel:

Name:

Place:

Date:

Time:

Tel:

Current medication(s) prescribed by your doctor

Medicine name:

Purpose:

Frequency & dose:

Start date:

End date:

Medicine name:

Purpose:

Frequency & dose:

Start date:

End date:

Medicine name:

Purpose:

Frequency & dose:

Start date:

End date:

Medicine name:

Purpose:

Frequency & dose:

Start date:

End date:

Other medicines/supplements you are taking, not prescribed by your doctor

Medicine/treatment:

Purpose:

Frequency & dose:

Start date:

End date:

Medicine/treatment:

Purpose:

Frequency & dose:

Start date:

End date:

Medicine/treatment:

Purpose:

Frequency & dose:

Start date:

End date:

Medicine/treatment:

Purpose:

Frequency & dose:

Start date:

End date:

Questions to ask at appointments
(Note: do bear in mind that doctors work under great time pressure, so long lists may not be helpful for either of you)

Questions to ask at appointments
(Note: do bear in mind that doctors work under great time pressure, so long lists may not be helpful for either of you)

Notes

Notes

Notes